Edtech
for the K-12 Classroom

ISTE Readings on How, When and Why to Use Technology

International Society for Technology in Education
PORTLAND, OREGON • ARLINGTON, VIRGINIA

Edtech for the K-12 Classroom: ISTE Readings on How, When and Why to Use Technology

Senior Editor: *Diana Fingal*
Managing Editor: *Emily Reed*
Copy Editor: *Julie Randles*
Cover Design: *Edwin Ouellette*
Ebook Production: *Stephanie Argy*

Library of Congress Cataloging-in-Publication Data available.

ISBN: 978-1-56484-693-8 (paperback)

Printed in the United States of America

ISTE® is a registered trademark of the International Society for Technology in Education.

About ISTE

The International Society for Technology in Education (ISTE) is the premier nonprofit organization serving educators and education leaders committed to empowering connected learners in a connected world. ISTE serves more than 100,000 education stakeholders throughout the world.

ISTE's innovative offerings include the ISTE Conference & Expo, one of the biggest, most comprehensive ed tech events in the world—as well as the widely adopted ISTE Standards for learning, teaching and leading in the digital age and a robust suite of professional learning resources, including webinars, online courses, consulting services for schools and districts, books, and peer-reviewed journals and publications. Visit iste.org to learn more.

Join Our Community of Passionate Educators

ISTE members get free year-round professional development opportunities and discounts on ISTE resources and conference registration. Membership also connects you to a network of educators who can instantly help with advice and best practices.

Join or renew your ISTE membership today! Visit http://iste.org/membership or call 800.336.5191.

About This Book

This book includes readings and other resources from the International Society for Technology in Education (ISTE), a global organization dedicated to harnessing technology to solve tough problems in education.

Designed to empower preservice teachers to use technology effectively in their classrooms and schools, the book is meant to supplement or replace a textbook. It is also designed to be used in tandem with ISTE membership, so future teachers can interact in robust professional learning networks, attend live webinars, gain access to online courses and read thought-provoking articles in *Empowered Learner*, ISTE's membership magazine.

To learn more about ISTE's offerings for higher education, and to download the instructor's guide for this book, visit iste.org/HigherEducation.

Other versions of this book come with membership included, so preservice students can use ISTE resources as part of their coursework. Although this version does not come embedded with ISTE membership, you can still sign up for a free one-year ISTE membership.

Visit iste.org/join to register for a basic membership. After filling out the required information, enter the code HIEDMEMBER at checkout. Contact iste@iste.org for assistance.

Contents

1   ISTE Standards 1

The ISTE Standards for Students are designed to empower student voice and ensure that learning is a student-driven process, and the ISTE Standards for Educators are your road map to helping students become empowered learners. These standards will deepen your practice, promote collaboration with peers, challenge you to rethink traditional approaches and prepare students to drive their own learning.

2   Support and Community 19

One of the most important assets teachers have is their colleagues. Why? Learning, collaborating and sharing is what turns good teachers into great teachers. It's also the foundation of the ISTE Standards for Educators, which invite educators of all types to "continually improve their practice by learning from and with others and exploring proven and promising practices that leverage technology to improve student learning."

Contents

3

Personalized Learning 35

Students have distinct learning needs, interests, aspirations and cultural backgrounds. Personalized learning is the idea that educators choose the strategy, content and even the environment that will best meet the needs of individual students. In doing so, they empower educators to solve the world's problems and become lifelong learners.

4

Digital Citizenship 59

Living and working in the digital age demands that all students act and model in ways that are safe, legal and ethical. But these days, digital citizenship is so much more than what not to do. Students need to feel empowered to create, to share, to solve, to collaborate and to connect with others in their classrooms and across the world.

5

Digital and Media Literacy 71

Digital and media literacy is all about accessing, analyzing, evaluating and creating all types of media, from newspaper and magazine articles to blog posts, tweets and YouTube videos. Having the skills to understand the intentions, biases and motives of the creator is essential in a world where manipulation of facts is easier than ever.empowered to create, to share, to solve, to collaborate and to connect with others in their classrooms and across the world.

6 Digital Equity 81

Digital equity is a giant umbrella covering different groups of people who depend on educators to advocate on their behalf to ensure every student can access the opportunities afforded by the digital age. Girls and people of color, students with disabilities, rural residents and those living in poverty often face barriers to access.

7 Digital Learning Lessons and Resources 97

There are endless edtech tools, methods and strategies you can choose from. As long as your lessons are aligned to the ISTE Standards, there are a variety of ways you can tailor your lessons to your students. The articles in this section offer a few examples of how you can use technology in a way that empowers learners and sets them up for success in their future careers and lives.

Foreword

I teach in an educator preparation program and see a large number of preservice teachers come through our doors and go out into the world to teach with little understanding about how to use technology to help facilitate learning. By the same token, they know even less about how to determine what works and doesn't work when it comes to using technology for learning. Not all my students feel lost with technology. Some of our graduates are very innovative with technology, and that gives me hope. But most still lack a basic understanding of why and how they should use technology in the K-12 classroom.

I teach a summer elective course called Educational Technology Methods, which introduces students to technology tools and resources, but only a handful of students are able to fit the class into their schedules. That's why this book, which offers easy-to-follow lessons and researched-based practices, is essential for all students in a teacher prep program—because using technology effectively in the classroom is no longer an option.

Too many educators are still swapping in new technology for old technology without tapping into the potential for these tools to foster personalized learning, global collaboration, problem-solving, critical-thinking and creation. For example, an administrator from a very large district in my area recently recalled observing a teacher who asked students to take out their classroom laptops and open up the e-textbook, and then called on a student to begin reading aloud.

It's not enough to let textbooks become e-textbooks, whiteboards become Smartboards or flashcards become flashcard apps. A basic understanding of how to use technology to support learning is of paramount importance.

We cannot just hand teacher's technology tools without giving them some resources to use them effectively. That's where this book comes in. In addition to readings and videos about specific ways to use technology for learning, this book offers three important ways educators can continue to improve their practice—not just now, but throughout their careers.

First, it offers a deep understanding of the ISTE Standards, a roadmap for how to transform education with technology.

Second, it introduces ways teachers can leverage technology to find ongoing, just-in-time professional development.

Third, it illustrates the importance and value of becoming aware and affiliated with professional development organizations like the International Society for Technology in Education.

I hope that you enjoy this book and find ideas you can use with your students immediately.

— **Jean Kiekel**,
Assistant professor at University of St. Thomas in Houston, Texas

1

ISTE Standards

In This Chapter:

The ISTE Standards for Students are designed to empower student voice and ensure that learning is a student-driven process, and the ISTE Standards for Educators are your road map to helping students become empowered learners. These standards will deepen your practice, promote collaboration with peers, challenge you to rethink traditional approaches and prepare students to drive their own learning.

The Student Standards are a suite of seven characteristics that reflect the skills students need to be successful in the world. They are: Empowered Learner, Digital Citizen, Knowledge Constructor, Innovative Designer, Computational Thinker, Creative Communicator and Global Collaborator. The Educator Standards are tied to the Student Standards and reflect seven characters that all educators should hone. They are: Learner, Leader, Citizen, Collaborator, Designer, Facilitator and Analyst.

The articles in this section will give you a sense of how to relate to these standards and how to practice and teach the skills necessary for working and living in the digital age.

Video: 7 Ways: The ISTE Standards for Students

Make learning with technology meaningful with the ISTE Standards for Students! Use this rap video produced by Flocabulary to learn more about the standards and share it with students to show them what it means to be a digital age learner.

The ISTE Standards for Students are a learner-driven process of exploration, creativity and discovery using technology for learning. Sing along using the lyrics below:

> Number one — I'm an Empowered Learner,
>
> I set goals and pursue 'em with fervor.
>
> My learning is up to me, it's not passive,

My brain learns best when I am digitally proactive,

 Number two — I'm a digital Citizen,

I stay safe on all the sites I'm visiting.

I use technology to make a difference

With power comes responsibility, you getting it?

I'm a Knowledge Constructor — number three,

I carefully select and evaluate what I read.

Curate media oh so brilliantly

(And) I think critically about source validity.

Four — I'm an Innovative Designer,

That means I solve problems, major and minor.

Start with empathy, ideate, then prototype,

Test and iterate, that method is so nice,

I'm a Computational Thinker — five,

Improving any process I can find.

Writing algorithms and testing in beta,

Analyzing to find the trends in the data.

I'm a Creative Communicator — (that's) six,

Like I put this in a rap song to make it stick.

I could use different media or tools,

Like infographics to make my point get through.

Seven — I'm a Global Collaborator,

I might connect with students way over the equator.

Digital technology makes the dream come true,

I had a virtual field trip with a kid in Peru.

That's seven ways that I can be

A life-long learner in this 21st century.

What kind of student do I want to be?

It's my path, that's up to me!

Teacher Empowerment Reflected in New Educator Standards

By Sarah Thomas

I had the pleasure of working on a team to refresh the ISTE Standards for Teachers, now known as the ISTE Standards for Educators. This team consisted of educators from many different roles, including perspectives from early childhood education, K-12 and higher education.

We spoke at length about framing the new standards to integrate seamlessly with the ISTE Standards for Students, emphasizing the power that teachers have individually and collectively to transform education. Several themes emerged, including teacher empowerment of professional learning, equity, transparency and active learning.

Teacher Empowerment of Professional Learning

Just as we advocate for choice in learning for our students, the same can be said of teachers. As professionals, we should be able to choose the professional learning path that will work best for our students. The new Learner standard encompasses all of these traits by recognizing our professionalism and encouraging us to set learning goals for ourselves.

Teachers are also encouraged to contribute to the field by sharing our experiences. This is where building a professional learning network (PLN), comprised of other educators around the world, comes into play. PLNs are powerful tools to bring out the best in each of us.

Equity

Equity in education is multifaceted, encompassing the quantity and quality of resources available to students. While some think of equity in the context of devices, there is much more involved. For example, students deserve equitable learning opportunities. Creativity in schools should not be limited to the more affluent districts. All learners deserve high-quality teachers who are motivated to grow professionally for the good of their students.

The new Educator Standards address equity in several areas, notably under the Leader, Collaborator, Designer and Facilitator standards.

As Leaders, teachers are charged to "advocate for equitable access to educational technology, digital content and learning opportunities to meet the diverse needs of all students." As Collaborators, we use the power of our networks to provide high-quality authentic learning experiences to prepare students for an increasingly global world. We meet the diverse needs of students through designing personalized learning experiences. Finally, as Facilitators, we nurture the creativity that all of our students bring to the table.

Transparency

One often-overlooked aspect of equity is the need to engage all stakeholders in our students' education. Many of the new standards focus on transparency, with the aspiration of partnering with parents and community members. There is also an increased focus in acknowledging the voices of the most important stakeholders of all, the learners themselves.

Transparency emerges as a theme in the Leader, Collaborator and Analyst standards. As Leaders, we must involve all stakeholders to make the best educational decisions for students, together. The Collaborator standard addresses the need to demonstrate cultural competency while communicating with students, parents and colleagues. All students and their families bring a wealth of cultural resources to our schools and classrooms that should be respected, appreciated and embraced. Finally, the Analyst standard focuses on using assessment data of all kinds, including those allowing for student creativity, to help guide students on their individual and collective learning journeys.

Active Learning

Relevance and authenticity are two things our learners crave. Many of our students aspire to create content, as opposed to passively consuming. Several ISTE standards promote student choice and voice in the classroom.

As Leaders, we aspire to help cultivate the creativity and inquiry of our learners. Through Citizenship, we model and promote responsible contributions to our connected digital world, opening learning beyond the walls of our schools. As Collaborators, we learn alongside our students and colleagues, working together to fuel learning.

The new ISTE Standards for Educators are aspirational and set a tone for what many of us hope to be. Not only do they support the ISTE Standards for Students, there are also connections with other frameworks, such as the National Education Technology Plan (NETP), Future Ready and many more.

Around the world, many educators have been buzzing about this rollout and what it means for the field. We, as educators, have so much power, both individually and collectively, that the new ISTE Standards for Educators have beautifully reflected.

This is an updated version of an article that was published in the July 2017 issue of Empowered Learner, ISTE's member magazine.

Sarah Thomas, Ph.D., is a regional technology coordinator in Prince George's County public schools. She is also the founder of the #edumatch movement, a project that empowers educators to make global connections across common areas of interest.

Dale Basye is the author of the books Personalized Learning: A Guide for Engaging Students with Technology, Get Active: Reimagining Learning Spaces for Student Success and the Circles of Heck series for Random House Children's books. He's interested in creative ways of personalizing learning to meet the diverse needs of today's students to help them become better equipped to deal with the challenges of the digital age workplace.

Tools to Support the ISTE Standards for Educators

By Kristin Harrington

The ISTE Standards for Educators challenge teachers to become leaders, creators and facilitators of dynamic or transformative student learning. What I love most about the standards is that they view educators as professionals who drive global change and continually reflect on their practice.

Great teachers understand the need to develop a network for support, resources and collaborative planning. They reach beyond their classroom walls to build a global network of educators in similar positions who have shared interests and who challenge their beliefs and ideas.

This article dives into a few of the ISTE Standards for Educators and the tools to support deepening your professional practice.

Building Your Global Network

The ISTE Standards for Educators offer a blueprint for building a global network. The Learner standard asks teachers to "pursue professional interests by creating and actively participating in local and global learning networks." The Collaborator standard elaborates on this, encouraging teachers to "dedicate time to collaborate with both colleagues and students to improve practice, discover and share resources and ideas, and solve problems."

When I started my career, teachers were just beginning to share ideas and resources in online forums. This type of collaboration eventually moved to social media sites such as Twitter, blogs and newer tools like Voxer and SnapChat.

Educators who embraced those tools quickly realized the many advantages of using social media tools to collaborate. You can jump on anytime of day or night, your network is global and the tools are free.

If you're just getting started, here are just a few of the tools and resources you can use to build a global network:

Give Twitter a try. If you haven't used Twitter, or only use it to follow celebrities, you might be skeptical about its power as a source for professional learning. Don't be. Every day, educators tweet thousands of fresh ideas and resources, collaborate on projects and support each other.

The trick is to learn how to use hashtags to find the information you're looking for so you can ignore what you don't need.

Whether you're interested in #PBL, #STEM or any other education topic, you cansearch the hashtag and find information on Twitter.

Don't like tweeting but want to find out what others are talking about? Join or follow an education Twitter chat, which is essentially a real-time discussion about a specific topic occurring during a set time. Participants use a unique hashtag so others can easily follow the chat.

You'll find a Twitter chat, or ed chat, for almost any subject area (#SciChat, #SSchat); job role (#CPChat); or education topic (#Spedchat, #digcit chat). Find a calendar of educational Twitter chats at participate.com/chats.

If you really love the tweets of a specific account, person or group of people, you can create a "list" of specific users. Still want to follow Kim K. and Beyonce? You can create a private list only you can see.

Check out Voxer. If lack of time is the reason you aren't networking with other educators, Voxer may be the tool for you. Voxer is a walkie-talkie app that educators use to have conversations about shared interests.

There are Voxer groups for podcasting in the classroom, makerspaces, edtech coaching and many other topics. You have the option of talking or typing, and you can listen while driving to and from work.

Although not totally private, Voxer is a lot less public than Twitter, making it a great forum for asking questions about things you're struggling with in your classroom or school.

Don't overlook edcamps. If you prefer face-to-face collaboration, edcamps may be your style of networking. These "unconferences" are organized by teachers and are offered in cities all over the world, with sessions chosen based on what participants want to learn or share that day.

Edcamps usually take place on Saturdays and include enthusiastic and innovative educators who are excited about sharing ideas and leave inspired to make changes in their classrooms. They also offer a great way to strengthen relationships with educators you collaborate with online.

Visit edcamp.org to find locations in your area. If you don't see one near you, consider gathering some colleagues to host an edcamp of your own.

Using Twitter and Voxer as well as attending edcamps has transformed my career by providing me with fresh ideas, inspiration and lifelong friends. And the more than 20 ISTE Professional Learning Networks will help you collaborate on the edtech topics you're interested in and connect with like-minded educators.

By breaking out of the bubble of your classroom or school, you're able to truly understand what's happening in education around the world and make the best decisions for your students.

Making the Most of the Leader Standard

While the Learner standard focuses on developing a global network, the Leader standard encourages educators to model for colleagues the identification, exploration, evaluation, curation and adoption of new digital resources and tools for learning.

If you've done any kind of search for classroom resources recently, you know there's no shortage of educational information and products online. And that's part of the problem. Evaluating learning materials can be overwhelming, time-consuming and frustrating. With a little organization and direction, however, you can find quality resources quickly and easily.

Here are a few resources to help you locate and curate resources:

Find Feedly. Full disclosure: I'm not an organized person. I was the student who had her desk dumped weekly and had to carefully open my locker so papers wouldn't cascade out.

Technology has saved me, and Feedly is one of my favorite tools for organizing and curating online content. With Feedly, you can add any blogs, online magazines or topics that you want to follow, creating a daily feed from all the sites you add.

You can categorize the sites and save your favorite posts for later, making it easy to stay up to date on educational trends. And everything stays in one place, ready for you to view when it's convenient for you.

Leverage your network. Now that you've established a network online, this is probably your most valuable resource for finding quality information and tools. Want to know what works for classroom management in a middle school classroom? Ask the question on Voxer or in an edcamp session. Need a resource for communicating with parents? Ask your Twitter friends what they use. My edupals have saved me many times, finding just the right answer to a question or the perfect resource for my classroom or to help a teacher.

Staying Current with the Learning Sciences

ISTE Educator Standard 1.c. encourages teachers to stay current with research that supports improved student learning outcomes, including findings from the learning sciences. It's no secret that teachers are under scrutiny and constantly evaluated based on choices they make in the classroom. Staying current with research and conducting action research in our classrooms empowers us to not only make the right decisions, but provides evidence to show why we made those decisions.

Here are a few resources to stay up on the learning sciences:

Go to Google Scholar. Google Scholar allows you to narrow your Google search results to journals and other scientific research, making it easier to find articles and educational studies. The searches often link to paid databases, so this is something to consider if you're looking for free resources.

Get decision-making help with the NMC Horizon Report. The New Media Consortium (NMC) publishes annual reports discussing current and future trends in education. Similar to Gartner's Hype Cycles, the NMC Horizon Report offers important information to help educators make decisions about purchases and initiatives in their classrooms and schools. Currently, there's a Horizon report for K-12 education, higher education, libraries and museums.

Visit the Office of Educational Technology's website. The U.S. Department of Education visits schools across the country to determine what's working and what isn't. Its website contains a wealth of research and publications that will help you effectively improve learning with technology in your classroom.

Read a report on ESSA and the future. The Center for Digital Education produced the "ESSA, Ed Tech, and the Future of Education" report in early 2017 about current practices and the future of Universal Design for Learning (UDL), blended learning, project-based learning and other educational topics.

By expanding your global network and curated resources, you're better equipped to begin exploring the other ISTE Standards for Educators. When you're ready to tackle Standard 5, Designer, by designing differentiated authentic learning opportunities, or to further develop your skills in facilitating authentic tasks with Standard 6, Facilitator, the work will be easier if you reach beyond your classroom walls and remember that you don't need to do it alone.

This is an updated version of an article that appeared in the January 2018 issue of Empowered Learner, ISTE's member magazine.

Kristin Harrington is a digital support colleague for Flagler County Public Schools in Florida. She's on the PLN leadership team for the ISTE Learning Spaces Network and is co-moderator of the Twitter chat #fledchat.

5 Ways to Help Students Become Innovative Designers

By Laura McLaughlin Taddei

Young children are naturally curious and creative, but they need adults who foster and encourage creativity, innovation and entrepreneurism.

In fact, the ISTE Standards for Educators remind us to "model and nurture creativity and creative expression to communicate ideas, knowledge or connections."

And as the ISTE Standards for Students spell out, when children become innovative designers, they have opportunities to think through problems and solve them by "creating new, useful or imaginative solutions."

Creativity, innovation and entrepreneurism build on each other to develop innovative designers who will become leaders continually looking for ways to solve problems and make a difference in their classrooms, homes and communities, and possessing the skills to bring their ideas to life.

Here are five tips for supporting young innovators:

1. Encourage Possibility Thinking

This type of thinking allows children to think through problems and move from what is to what might be. Asking questions like, "What can you try that you haven't done before?" or "What if you changed a part of it?" or "What would you do if you knew you wouldn't fail?" or "How is this problem like another problem?" or "What is the environment that this problem exists in and how might we make our problem responsive to that environment?" This thinking inspires careful risk-taking, problem-solving and a mindset that anything is possible.

2. Teach Systematic Inventive Thinking

Inside-the-box thinking, aka Systematic Inventive Thinking (SIT) as described by Drew Boyd and Jacob Goldenberg, provides a simple way for anyone to be innovative using one of five templates (subtraction, division, multiplication, task unification and attribute dependency). Once young children learn this simple process for creativity, they can use it for a lifetime and be innovators in all they do.

Ask students to think of an ordinary object they like to use and then share some things they can change about this item (components, features and functions). Ask what are some things they cannot change (environmental, physical factors)? What changes could they make (use one of five SIT templates)? And how would these changes be beneficial?

3. Create an Explore and Take-Apart Station

Young children can benefit not only from their teachers support in fostering creativity, innovation and entrepreneurism, but also their families' support. One way to engage families in supporting young innovators is to ask them to donate old household items that can be used for exploration. Think old computers, cell phones, umbrellas and PVC pipe. Use the materials to create a "tinkering" station where students can safely take apart items and be inspired to get creative, innovate and solve problems.

4. Provide Prop Boxes and Engage in Role Play

Stocking the classroom with boxes of props and allowing students to engage in different roles provides them with authentic learning experiences where they can explore, imagine and think through problems. Adding a digital camera or iPad so children can take pictures and video their experiences to later reflect on them or create a story to share with others would also inspires young innovators.

5. Help Students Set Personal Goals

Empowering children to set personal goals and guiding them to resources where they can explore passions will help them to become self-directed and self-motivated learners. Children can create action plans and, even before writing, they can draw pictures of their goals and passions. The earlier we integrate goal setting and action planning, the more we inspire children to be creative, innovative, young entrepreneurs.

When young children are passionate and excited about their ideas, they will continue to think creatively, problem-solve and develop as innovative designers. Children who are creative, innovative and possess an entrepreneurial mindset hopefully grow into adults who are open-minded, flexible, self-directed problem-solvers who will contribute positively to their communities and society.

This is an updated version of an article that published on the ISTE Blog on September 13, 2017.

Laura McLaughlin Taddei is an associate professor of education at Neumann University in Aston, Pennsylvania, and a professional development speaker in higher education and PK-12 settings. She is dedicated to teaching and modeling the use of innovation, creativity, critical thinking, communication and collaboration both within the classroom setting and beyond.

4 Myths (and 4 Truths) About Empowered Learners

By Sarah Stoeckl, Jody Britten and Cheryl Lemke

In a world of rapid change, the ultimate goal of education should be deep, authentic learning that prepares students for life in a global, high-tech society.

This learning can be amplified and supported through strategies and practices that empower learners.

When learners are empowered they have meaningful opportunities to use their voice and make choices related to their full learning experience. When empowered, students can engage in the deep learning that supports long-term academic success and true learning (instead of memorization) and mastery of learning objectives.

Lack of Empowerment = Surface Learning

When students aren't empowered, decisions are made for them and learning opportunities are directed and controlled. Research shows that when students experience this lack of empowerment, they engage in more surface learning, where they do just enough to meet teachers' expectations.

What does it actually mean to empower learners in practice? Educators in today's classrooms, leaders in today's schools and districts, families of today's students and even students themselves often misinterpret the idea of empowered learners.

Myths and Truths About Empowered Learning

Here are the top four myths about empowering learners:

Myth 1: Empowering learners requires strategies that aren't tied to the current goals of my school or district.

Truth 1: The research base for learner empowerment is tied directly to instructional approaches that are on the radar of any contemporary learning organization.

Whether the approach is differentiated, personalized or even problem-based learning, these contemporary best practices all support learner empowerment.

Efforts toward empowerment can be supported through just about any effective, research-based instructional choice that is focused on deep, authentic learning.

Myth 2: I differentiate therefore I empower learners.

Truth 2: Differentiation can happen at many different levels and the strategies that support the differentiation of instruction can support the true empowerment of learners.

Research shows that differentiation that increases motivation, engagement and participation in the learning process can improve student academic success.

However, it's not enough to just differentiate materials, processes or products. Learner empowerment is nurtured through environment, planning, access to digital resources, opportunities to solve complex problems, engagement with real-world issues, and applying analysis and critical thinking skills.

Empowering learners has just as much to do with staging situational factors as it does with being transparent about the planning, design and facilitation choices teachers make for and with their classroom.

Myth 3: I will lose all control if I really empower learners in my classroom.

Truth 3: An empowered learner has a lot to do with the empowering behaviors of his or her teacher. In the empowered classroom, teachers change their focus away from control and toward facilitation.

These teachers foster engagement, motivation and self-direction of their students. These educators rethink the very idea of control, giving more autonomy to students, both individually and in groups, while sustaining their goal to manage and create a safe, effective learning environment.

Empowering teachers understand the nuances and complexity that allow them to be responsible educators within this new mindset while scaffolding students in opportunities to have choice, use their individual voices, and engage in purposeful, meaningful and relevant learning.

Myth 4: All students are ready to be empowered learners.

Truth 4: Yes, all students have the capacity to be empowered learners. The key question to ask is if they are all immediately ready to be empowered learners. The answer is, quite simply, no.

Students need the time and support to prepare and develop the skills of empowered learners. They need to have an understanding of why they should be empowered in their learning.

They should have strategies to engage in critical thinking and analysis. They should have opportunities to practice, fail, retry and re-strategize about their learning, success, goal attainment, engagement, etc.

Empowerment doesn't happen overnight; students need to develop the foundational skills and understanding so that they can connect their learning experiences into a solid foundation for being empowered learners.

Students need to have the vocabulary, understanding, skills and strategies to practice and perfect their empowerment. Once students are prepared to be empowered learners, they need safe places to practice and participate before they can be fully, continuously empowered.

The takeaway is that teachers are even more crucial in an empowering learner environment, and their role is all the more complex and interesting.

While it may seem like a burden or an extra "thing to do" for educators to work toward developing students as empowered learners, the result is an outcome that all educational organizations strive for: college-, career- and life-ready individuals who are able to contribute to the diverse, digital and dynamic world in which they live.

This is an updated version of an article published on the ISTE Blog on August 23, 2017.

Sarah Stoeckl is a senior project manager in the ISTE Standards Department. She worked as a writing and literature teacher before becoming an administrator, writer and project wrangler.

Jody Britten, Ph.D., is a senior associate at Metiri Group assisting educational stakeholders in the use of research-based strategies and tools to advance digital learning in PK-20.

Cheryl Lemke is president and CEO of the Metiri Group, a consulting firm dedicated to advancing effective uses of technology in education.

Educator Standards Slideshare

Stretch your edtech practice with this slideshare featuring the ISTE Standards for Educators.

**https://www.slideshare.net/ISTE/
stretch-your-edtech-practice-with-the-iste-standards-for-educators**

To learn more about the ISTE Standards, visit iste.org/standards. Here are some additional resources for learning about the standards and how they can inform learning and teaching.

ISTE Standards for Students: A Practical Guide for Learning with Technology.
STE members save 25% at iste.org/StudentStandards.

ISTE Standards for Educators: A Guide for Teachers and Other Professionals.
ISTE members save 25% at iste.org/EducatorStandards.

2

Support and Community

In This Chapter:

One of the most important assets teachers have is their colleagues. Why? Learning, collaborating and sharing is what turns good teachers into great teachers. It's also the foundation of the ISTE Standards for Educators, which invite educators of all types to "continually improve their practice by learning from and with others and exploring proven and promising practices that leverage technology to improve student learning."

That not only means getting advice from a subject-area colleague, it also involves learning with others from around your community and around the world. Attend an edcamp, join a Twitter chat, crowdsource a question with your professional learning network.

The selections in this section will help redefine what professional learning is all about in the digital age.

Organize an Edcamp for Your District

By Janet Warden and Caroline Pidala

How do the teachers in your school react when you schedule a professional learning day? If they are less than enthusiastic, it might be time to ask yourself if you're doing it right.

Don't get us wrong — we understand. We've been educators and administrators at districts where training seemed a necessary chore at best. But at Wappingers Central School District in Hopewell Junction, New York, we wanted to do better. That's why we embarked on a strategic planning initiative that included making our professional learning days as collaborative and engaging as possible. The solution we hit on — proposed by district technology integration specialists Paul Rubeo and Daniel Roberto — was a districtwide edcamp.

Edcamps are organic, participant-driven professional learning experiences created by teachers, for teachers. They are built around the simple structure of teachers teaching each other what they know — collaborative learning at its best. They strive to bring teachers together to talk about the things that matter most to them: their interests, passions and questions. With this spirit in mind, we launched EdcampWCSD.

Our results were nothing short of phenomenal. Teachers got into the spirit almost immediately, tweeting about their excitement and what they were learning before, during and after the event.

"A prof dev day that leaves me refreshed, inspired and ready to try new things!" said one.

"Sharing across buildings, across disciplines — great day!!" said another.

"We have been inspired by the best!"

Although this was our first edcamp, it was a huge success, largely due to our concerted planning, from the promotional stages through execution. Here's how we did it.

Promoting the Edcamp

Because collaboration lies at the center of the edcamp approach, we knew we had to drum up as much participation and excitement as possible and get our teachers — who would be both the educators and the students at our edcamp — involved as early as possible.

Here are the tools we used to promote the event:

Website. We kicked off our edcamp planning efforts by launching a website two months before the event. We sent the link out on Twitter and social channels. Eventually, we put survey links, the edcamp schedule, tutorials and other resources on the site.

Video tutorials. We posted video tutorials on the website explaining the role of session facilitators and the backchanneling process, which allows people participating remotely to interact in the conversation via Twitter or other videoconferencing tools. This was as much of a promotional tactic as a logistical one. It showed participants that this was a big deal and it fueled their enthusiasm.

Twitter. We helped educators at each school set up Twitter accounts if they didn't already have them. We created the hashtag #EdcampWCSD and encouraged everyone to tweet photos of their preparation and share their excitement with their professional learning networks.

Google Forms survey. We created a survey to find out what session topics resonated with faculty, staff and administrators. We asked administrators to help spread the word by inviting their staffs to help shape the event. It worked. We received over 650 responses.

We also asked survey takers for their grade level, department, building assignments and interest in facilitating sessions. This data automatically populated a Google Sheet for easy analysis. The Professional Development Committee and administration reviewed all survey results and worked to consolidate sessions, finalize titles and make recommendations for session facilitators.

Planning the Event

Our district is large, so we put on three separate edcamps — for primary, intermediate and secondary levels.

We ended up with 212 sessions on a wide range of edtech topics, from using interactive whiteboards to tech tools for formative assessment. The final schedule went up on the website with a link to another Google Form for registration that asked participants to select 10-12 sessions in four time slots. We offered the most popular sessions multiple times to meet demand.

We then sorted information from the session selection survey to create participant lists for each topic. With access to the Google Sheets, each principal could track the registration progress. Once registration was complete, we sent a link to a document posted on the website listing participants and the room number for each session.

Preparing the Facilitators

We gave each facilitator video tutorials and a text document offering tips and guidance on facilitating sessions. Each facilitator was responsible for creating a Google Doc for their session and adding information before the event to help generate conversation on the topic.

We asked facilitators to remind attendees to share specific examples and resources, and we encouraged them to acknowledge and engage participants using Twitter as a backchannel. At the end of each session, we asked that they allow all participants five minutes to drop everything and tweet.

The success of each session depended on the contributions of its participants. The facilitator's job was not to make a presentation but to keep the discussion moving.

Collaborating on the Big Day

When the day of the WCSD Edcamp arrived — a Friday at the end of March — we were ready. At each of the three locations, the day kicked off with an opening session about the importance of teacher leadership and becoming a connected educator.

We promoted backchanneling using the Twitter hashtag, which fed into a live feed, as well as capturing the "big ideas" from each session in Google Docs to create a digital archive. Over 700 faculty, staff and administrators participated in the WCSD Edcamp. Some of their favorite sessions included:

- Google: Yes, It Is Really More Than a Search Engine
- Growth Mindset
- Using Technology for Formative Assessments
- 80/20 Genius Hour: Using Students' Passions to Motivate Learning
- Merging Content Across STEM
- Can We Talk About Race

Although some facilitators were nervous at first, they soon discovered that moments after the clock started on their 45-minute sessions, the ideas were flowing and the conversation was lively.

One of the best tools of the event was the live feed, which enabled teachers around the district to interact during their sessions. Most found it exhilarating to collaborate with far-flung colleagues. At the end of the edcamp, participants reflected on the event in a "smackdown" session. Overall, teachers and administrators loved the opportunity to meet with their colleagues and exchange information and ideas.

Keeping the Learning Going

We also sent out a feedback survey. Here are just a few things that participants had to say about the experience:

"Edcamp helped to build my confidence and helped my area of knowledge."

"Giving everyone the same voice was empowering."

"Hearing from teaching assistants to administration and everyone in between on the same topics was inspiring."

To extend the professional learning beyond this day, we continued adding resources and comments to the interactive documents. The Google Docs became a tool for collaboration and a catalogued professional development resource for the district.

Our edcamp experience has taught us that, much like students, educators learn best when they have a choice. When you ask educators what they want to learn about, you cultivate a climate where everyone is focused on positive, ongoing growth and student achievement.

This is an updated version of an article that published on the ISTE Blog on December 23, 2015.

Caroline Pidala is principal of Millbrook High School in New York. She was formerly an assistant principal at Roy C. Ketcham High School in Wappingers Central School District.

Janet Warden is the assistant superintendent for curriculum and personnel at the Carmel Central School District. She was formerly the assistant superintendent for curriculum and instruction at the Wappingers Central School District.

Twitter is Dumb! Or is It?

By Jaime Donally

"Twitter is dumb; no one uses it!" Those were the first words out of my mouth the first time I was told to use the social network for a tech conference.

I wasn't opposed to using social media as a collaboration tool, I just couldn't get past the fact that most of my friends only used Facebook. Does anyone really want to be limited by 140 (now 280) characters? Not me! Or so I thought.

Back then, I was transitioning from classroom teaching to instructional technology. In my first year, I was expected to support classroom teachers in all subjects, which required hours of Google Search. You could say that my professional learning network (PLN) consisted of keeping my fingers crossed hoping to run across the right resources from the top experts.

All that began to change when I decided to put my opinions about Twitter to the test. In preparing for the school year, I had to list three measurable goals for professional growth, and I chose to make one of those goals about Twitter. That way I could see for myself if using the microblogging tool would lead to my professional growth and, at the same time, benefit my technology department.

Specifically, my Twitter goal was to post five times a week. It seemed like a daunting commitment given all my other tasks. But little did I know that what seemed like an ambitious goal would turn out to be easy – and a bit addicting.

From the beginning, I enjoying finding and sharing resources on Twitter, but it was something else that got me hooked. One evening, I stumbled upon a Twitter chat. At first, I couldn't understand why so many responses were using the same odd hashtag in their conversations. Then I realized that this was a chat – a group of likeminded people from around the world coming together to discuss a topic of interest to all of them.

That date, Feb. 12, 2012, is now etched in my memory as the moment when my Twitter world was unleashed and my addiction to Twitter chats began.

I realized that I could learn more in one Twitter chat than I did during a week-long conference or from my endless hours of Google searches. I began to wonder why more teachers were not engaging with these chats. How did I hit the jackpot by connecting with these #edtech experts?

I became obsessed with sharing this incredible tool with other educators. As a Hoonuit contributor, I created modules on Building a PLN, Connecting Globally and also a module for students on Live Video Streaming using social media. I have even leveraged Twitter to host global events, such as #GlobalMakerDay.

And I run a weekly Twitter chat on augmented and virtual reality in education #ARVRinEDU.

I think all educators have a personal desire for growth. And the ISTE Standards for Educators advise us to "pursue professional interests by creating and actively participating in local and global learning networks." Twitter offers you an opportunity to do just that, and it's free and easy.

If you're ready to start using Twitter to build a PLN, here are six tips to get you started:

1. Get serious and get scheduled. Jumping into Twitter on occasion is no better than searching for something on Google. The point of social media is to be social and that takes consistency. It may seem uncomfortable at first, but make an effort to be on Twitter at least five times a week.

2. Collaborate. One of the greatest benefits of social media is the opportunity to collaborate with others around the world. Sharing information is just as important as validating information you find with "retweets." Don't be afraid to thank educators for valuable resources or ask questions to get support. Collaboration connects your personal learning to a network that forms your PLN.

3. Understand hashtags and handles. There's a difference between #hashtags and @handles. The purpose of a hashtag is to collaborate and search for a specific topic, as in the post, "I am thrilled to share at #ISTE18 this summer on the topics of #AR and #VR." If I wanted the ISTE Twitter account to get notified of my post, I would write, "I am thrilled to share at #ISTE18 this summer! Thank you @ISTE for the opportunity." Since ISTE uses the Twitter account @ISTE, they're notified each time a post mentions that handle.

4. Connect. There are many different strategies around whom you should follow or not follow. The purpose of following educators and #edtech leaders on Twitter is to learn from their posts. Be intentional about who you follow because it's their posts you will see in your Twitter feed. We all start with friends when joining social media, so let's connect! You can find me on Twitter as @jaimedonally.

5. Join a Twitter chat. Although I landed in my first Twitter chat by accident, having a strategy when joining in is more likely to get you hooked. Find a chat that offers the topics that you enjoy sharing or learning about. Many times, we're limited by our availability to be on social media, so we pick chats that fit in our schedule. Fortunately, jumping into a chat also gives you a group of educators who want to help you.

6. Follow the chat protocol. The most important part of a Twitter chat is using the same #hashtag in all your responses so that everyone in the chat can see your answers. The moderator will give you a Q1, Q2 for questions while you and others will respond with A1, A2 for answers.

My most-valued reward for taking the social media plunge are my global connections #eduheroes. While many of my friends remained on Facebook to talk about their latest adventures and family announcements, I've taken a journey into building new friendships with my personal learning network.

I was wrong! Twitter is not dumb, and every day I use it for my professional growth.

This is an updated version of an article that originally published on the ISTE Blog on March 17, 2017.

Jaime Donally, a passionate technology enthusiast, began her career as a math teacher and eventually taught students in PK-8. She is the author of the ISTE book *Learning Transported.*

Get the Most out of Twitter Chats

By Alyssa Korinke

Are you a connected educator? Whether you have a professional learning network (PLN) in your school or you link up via social media, connection is the key to innovation and growth as an educator. Twitter — and Twitter chats in particular — have become an effective way to build those networks and share your learning. With its own set of rules and jargon, a Twitter chat can be intimidating and tough to track. Follow these tips and you'll be tweeting like a pro in no time.

1. What Exactly Is a Twitter Chat?

A Twitter chat is a conversation in real time connecting people from all over the globe who want to talk about a specific topic. Using a hashtag you can follow the conversation on Twitter or on other applications like TweetDeck or TweetChat. Typically these chats last an hour and consist of six to eight questions posted by the host account and answered by participants.

Pro tip: Use the hashtag in every tweet.

Pro tip: A Twitter chat is a conversation, so don't just answer the questions. Feel free to ask questions and comment on posts from other participants. If the chat is moving too quickly, just focus on a couple of users and interact directly with them.

2. Who Participates?

Twitter chats are most often hosted by PLNs, corporate accounts or other organizations and have a specific focus or theme. Educators can participate in chats specific to learning models, areas of interest, geographical location or even specific districts. While it's nearly impossible to keep up with the proliferation of chats, you can find a fairly extensive list here.

Pro tip: Participate regularly in a chat or two to build thought leadership and create connections.

Pro tip: Don't want to miss tweets from a specific #eduhero or your PLN? Create a Twitter list of the thought leaders you want to follow.

3. How Do I Get Started?

The conversation moves very quickly, but don't let that intimidate you. There are several tools like TweetDeck or TweetChat to help organize the feed and more easily navigate the chat.

Use multiple streams or feeds to monitor the host Twitter account, the hashtag and your own mentions simultaneously. Toggling between windows or streams cuts down on confusion from having to search the hashtag each time you check your notifications.

Pro tip: Replying to tweets will link them in a conversation, even if you delete the @mention.

Pro tip: After the chat, reply to each person who mentioned you or commented on your tweets to further build your network.

This is an updated version of an article that first appeared on the ISTE Blog on Sept. 12, 2016.

Alyssa Korinke is a social media strategist who manages the many social channels at ISTE. Her passion for connecting physical and digital environments has brought a new perspective to ISTE's digital spaces and the conference experience since 2016.

40 Education Twitter Chats Worth Your Time

By Diana Fingal

For educators who thrive on connections, Twitter chats may be the perfect form of professional development. They're free. They focus on just the topic you need. They happen regularly. And they give you access to an instant community, complete with networking opportunities, emotional support and the chance to give back.

Participating in chats even aligns with the ISTE Standards for Educators because they allow you to improve your practice by learning from and with others to explore proven and promising practices that leverage technology to improve student learning.

"The collective intelligence of a chat can provide educators with classroom-tested lessons, a variety of perspectives on specific problems or an introduction to emerging technologies," says Daniel Krutka (@dankrutka), who uses Twitter to connect to his students and the rest of the education community. "Chats also offer leaders opportunities to expand their audiences and influence, and they give voice to teachers who might not otherwise have the chance to exercise leadership outside their classrooms or schools."

But with hundreds of ed-related chats, how do you know which ones are worth giving up an hour of your day?

First, pick your angle. Some chats, such as #edchat, tackle a broad range of education issues, while others are based on shared interests in a particular topic, content area, grade level, job type or geographical region. Next, try out a couple that fit your criteria and see which community you feel most at home in.

To get you started, check out this list of 41 education chats curated by the ISTE community, organized by chat type. If you don't find something for you on this list, check out Participate.com, which hosts an easy to use list of chats organized by topic and even highlights happening each day.

General Education Chats

#edchat (Thursdays, 4 p.m. PT/7 p.m. ET) One of the first education chats, this popular chat has nine moderators and covers a broad range of topics. Find upcoming topics and read archived chats at edchat.pbworks.com.

#engchat (Monday, 4 p.m. PT/7 p.m. ET) Where English teachers share ideas, resources and inspiration.

#ISTEchat (Third Thursday, 5 p.m. PT/8 p.m. ET) Focuses on issues related to edtech and the ISTE Standards.

#nt2t (Saturdays, 6 a.m. PT/9 a.m. ET) For educators who are new to Twitter.

#OK2Ask (every other Thursday, 5 p.m. PT/8 p.m. ET) Friendly chat with lots of classroom resources shared.

#satchat (Saturdays, 4:30 a.m. PT/7:30 a.m. ET) For current and emerging school leaders, #satchat became so popular it spawned two geographically specific offshoot chats: #SatchatWC for West Coasters and #SatchatOC for educators living in Oceania (Indonesia, Polynesia, Australia, New Zealand, Singapore, etc.).

Job Role Chats

#1stchat (Sunday, 5 p.m. PT/8 p.m. ET) Chat about first grade teaching.

#cpchat (Wednesdays, 5 p.m. PT/8 p.m. ET) For connected principals and those interested in school leadership.

#ETCoaches The ISTE Edtech Coaches Network hosts book study slow chats where educators focus on a new book for four to six weeks. Check out the calendar for info.

#kinderchat (Mondays, 6 p.m. PT/9 p.m. ET) For anyone interested in kindergarten and early-childhood education.

#mschat (Thursdays at 5 p.m. PT/8 p.m. ET) For middle school teachers.

Topical Chats

#AR4Learning (Thursdays, 6 p.m. PT/9 p.m. ET) Focused on augmented reality in the classrooms.

#ARVRinEDU (Wednesdays, 6 p.m. PT/9 p.m. ET) Discussion about augmented and virtual reality in education.

#BookCreator chat (Last Thursday of the month, 11 a.m. PT/2 p.m. ET) Over the course of the chat, participants collaborate on a book and publish it online.

#digcit (Wednesdays, 4 p.m. PT/7 p.m. ET) Focuses on digital citizenship. Read the chat archives on the #digcit website.

#EdTechChat (Mondays, 5 p.m. PT/8 p.m. ET) Focuses on topics related to edtech.

#FlipClass (Mondays, 5 p.m. PT/8p.m. ET) For those interested in the flipped classroom model.

#formativechat (Mondays, 4:30 p.m. PT/7:30 p.m. ET) Discussion of topics related to formative assessment, from giving effective feedback to giving students more ownership of their learning.

#Games4Ed (Thursdays, 5 p.m. PT/8 p.m. ET; Sundays, noon PT/3 p.m. ET) For those interested in game-based learning and gamification.

#iteachphysics (Saturdays, 6 a.m. PT/ 9 a.m. ET) Bi-weekly chat for physics teachers.

#kidscancode (Tuesdays, 5 p.m. PT/8 p.m. ET) For educators interested in helping students learn to program.

#LearnLAP (Mondays, 5 p.m, PT/ 8 p.m. ET) Focuses on strategies for creating a student-led classroom.

#pblchat (Tuesdays, 6 p.m. PT/9 p.m. ET) For project-based learning fans.

#PersonalizedPD (Tuesdays, 6 p.m. PT/ 9 p.m. ET) For those interested in customizing professional development to meet the needs of each educator.

#plearnchat (Mondays, 4 p.m. PT/7 p.m. ET) Topics focus on personalized learning, learner agency, changing culture, voice and choice, and strategies to transform teaching and learning.

#Read4fun (Every other Sunday, 4 p.m. PT/7 p.m. ET) Connects passionate educators with books, and with each other.

#Shiftthis (Tuesdays, 5 p.m. PT/8 p.m. ET) Focuses on implementing gradual change for massive impact in the classroom.

#sschat (Mondays, 4 p.m. PT, 7 p.m. ET) For social studies educators.

#TLAP (Mondays, 6 p.m. PT/9 p.m. ET) For educators who embrace David Burgess' approach of teaching like a pirate.

#WeirdEd (Wednesdays, 7 p.m. PT/10 p.m. ET) Focuses on positive issues, taking action and the kids.

#whatisschool (Thursdays, 5 p.m. PT/8 p.m. ET) Educators discuss shaping the future of school.

#XPLAP (Tuesdays, 5 p.m. PT/8 p.m. ET) Based on Explore Like a Pirate, chat focuses on gamification.

Regional Chats

#bcedchat (Sunday, 7 p.m. PT/10 p.m. ET) For educators in the British Columbia area. Find a list of archived chats on the website.

#CAedchat (Sundays, 8 p.m. PT/11 p.m. ET) California educators discuss education topics relevant to the West Coast.

#NCed (Tuesdays, 5 p.m. PT/8 p.m. ET) For North Carolina educators.

#UrbanEdChat (Thursdays, 7 p.m. PT/ 10 p.m. ET) For educators who want to discuss urban education.

@UTedChat (Wednesdays, 8 p.m. PT/11 p.m. ET) Focuses on education topics relevant to Utah and the general education landscape.

This is an updated version of an article published on the ISTE Blog on May 19, 2015.

Diana Fingal is ISTE's director of editorial content.

Video: Sarah Thomas on Building a Personal Learning Family

Learning comes naturally to educators, but in today's busy world, it can be hard to prioritize time for learning. In her Ignite talk at ISTE 2017, Sarah Thomas reminds educators of how empowering and important it is to connect and share with one another.

She shares her thoughts and insights on building a personal learning network (PLN), or what she refers to as her "Personal Learning Family," and discusses how powerful educators are when they come together and support one another. When they do, they benefit their students as well as themselves.

Learner is one of the new ISTE Standards for Educators, and embodying the Learner is an important part of honing your educational practice and working toward a world where all learners thrive, achieve and contribute.

Watch the video at the following link to hear more from Sarah Thomas.

www.youtube.com/watch?v=lTqApfP_4ik&feature=youtu.be

Video: How to Survive Your First Year of Teaching

Your first year of teaching can be exciting and rewarding, but it can also be overwhelming and confusing. Watch the video for five survival tips for new and first-year teachers from the ISTE Young Educator Network.

The ISTE Young Educator Network is a vibrant community of both new and veteran teachers under 35 who are passionate about transforming learning through the meaningful use of edtech. They are innovative, generous and dedicated professionals who love to share resources, grow their PLNs and support one another.

Watch the video at **www.youtube.com/watch?v=Be-Woe3h_po&feature=youtu.be**

Resources

Here are some suggestions for joining the conversation around edtech.

Follow @ISTE on Twitter and tune into an upcoming #ISTEchat for different perspectives on timely topics.

Post a question to the ISTE Communities. Check out the different forums for discussion at community.iste.org.

3

Personalized Learning

In This Chapter:

Students have distinct learning needs, interests, aspirations and cultural backgrounds. Personalized learning is the idea that educators design the strategy, content and even the environment that will best meet the needs of individual students.

Author Dale Basye defines personalized learning as "learning that is tailored to the preferences and interests of various learners, as well as instruction that is paced to a student's unique needs. Academic goals, curriculum and content — as well as method and pace — can all conceivably vary in a personalized learning environment."

Personalized learning environments allow students to meet the ISTE Standards for Students, which call on learners to "leverage technology to take an active role in choosing, achieving and demonstrating competency in their learning goals, informed by the learning sciences."

The selections in this section define personalized learning in greater detail and provide examples of what it looks like in action. Don't miss the inspiring video of Katharine Hale explaining how to empower students by changing their stories.

Personalized vs. Differentiated vs. Individualized Learning

By Dale Basye

Words are meaningless unless all concerned agree on their specific definitions. Even if there is a general consensus on terms, what those terms actually mean in the real world has a tendency to evolve and morph without warning.

Nowhere is this more prevalent than in the field of education. In fact, there are so many "terms du jour" thrown around, tweeted and traded these days that their intrinsic value is often questionable, and confusing. Take the terms differentiated, individualized and personalized. What can we make of these three near-synonyms? Short answer: Plenty!

Modern classrooms are teeming with students of varying interests, backgrounds, abilities and learning needs. To engage these students, learning must be every bit as diverse as they are. In the ISTE/Intel Education book Personalized Learning: A Guide for Engaging Students with Technology (which I wrote with my colleague, Peggy Grant. Ph.D.), we teased out the crucial nuances that distinguish these terms in an attempt to demystify the approaches they refer to so that educators may better initiate more effective learning techniques.

Differentiated Learning

Within the context of education, differentiation is a type of learning where instruction is tailored to meet the learning needs, preferences and goals of individual students. The overarching academic goals for groups of students are the same, yet the teacher has the latitude to use whatever resources and approaches he or she sees fit to connect with a student or use practices that have proved successful for similar students in the past.

Regardless of what a teacher decides to differentiate — whether it's subject matter, the learning process or even the environment where learning occurs — differentiation is an awareness of and active response to students' varied learning needs. It involves exercising flexibility in assessment, grouping and instruction to create the best learning experience possible.

Here's how differentiation works: A teacher responds to a student's unique learning needs through the learning process, the educational content or the specific learning vehicle or product, based on a student's interests, learning profile or readiness.

According to Jennipher Willoughby, a freelance writer and former science and technology specialist for Lynchburg City Schools in Lynchburg, Virginia, teachers differentiate by providing different paths to learning that help students make sense of concepts and skills. They also provide appropriate levels of challenge for all students, no matter their competency. Conversely, teachers do not differentiate by developing a separate lesson plan for each student in a classroom or by merely "watering down" the curriculum for some students.

It's about connecting the dots: linking the academic goals of the curriculum with students' diverse interests and capacities. This takes really knowing the students in your classroom and adapting your curriculum where possible. This also requires the development of a comprehensive plan for how you will use resources and how much time it takes to facilitate differentiated learning and to assess results.

Individualized Learning

Instruction calibrated to meet the unique pace of various students is known as individualized learning. If differentiation is the "how" then individualization is the "when." The academic goals, in this case, remain the same for a group of students, but individual students can progress through the curriculum at different speeds, based on their own particular learning needs. This approach serves students who may need to review previously covered material, students who don't want to waste time covering information they've already mastered, or students who need to proceed through the curriculum more slowly or immerse themselves in a certain topic or principle to really "get" it.

The term individualized instruction was coined nearly 50 years ago. Initially, the approach included any teaching strategies that met an individual student's needs, but — in practice — the term describes students working through set materials or curricula at their own rates. With individualized instruction, learning strategies are based on student readiness, interests and best practices. All of this is meant to help each student master the skills they will need as defined by established academic standards.

Personalized Learning

Perhaps the most confusing term of them all is personalized learning. Some misuse the term, thinking it refers to a student's choice of how, what and where they learn according to their preferences. Others confuse it with individualization, taking it as a reference to lessons that are paced at different rates to accommodate different students.

Really, personalized learning — at least in our understanding of the term — refers to the whole enchilada: learning that is tailored to the preferences and interests of various learners, as well as instruction that is paced to a student's unique needs. Academic goals, curriculum and content — as well as method and pace — can all conceivably vary in a personalized learning environment.

Unlike individualized instruction, personalized learning involves the student in the creation of learning activities and relies more heavily on a student's personal interests and innate curiosity. Instead of education being something that happens to the learner, it is something that occurs as a result of what the student is doing, with the intent of creating engaged students who have truly learned how to learn.

This method is obviously a far cry from the way that most teachers are traditionally trained to interact with students. Personalization, in addition to responding to students' needs and interests, teaches them to manage their own learning — to take control and ownership of it. It's not something that is done to them but something that they participate in doing for themselves. For teachers, personalized learning is about facilitation more than dissemination.

Since the most effective (and unrealistic) application of true personalized learning would require one-on-one tutoring for every student based on their interests, preferences, needs and pace, personalized learning is often conceived of as an instructional method that incorporates adaptive technology to help all students achieve high levels of learning.

Putting It all Together

Technology — when employed properly and meaningfully — can help educators deliver differentiated, individualized and personalized instruction. It can help facilitate timely interventional responses, involve parents more in their children's learning, empower school leaders with data to support teachers, and either break down problems or make those problems more complex, based on the individual needs of the student. It's up to savvy teachers to connect the appropriate tools with the right students — and, in the case of personalized learning, allowing students to make suggestions and control their own academic experiences.

Modern learning is the ultimate collaboration between teacher and student. Much like a doctor, the teacher must assess each individual's needs, then prescribe the right solution for that person by crafting an appropriate curriculum and delivering it in a way that is meaningful. At the same time, students know on some level what teaching-learning style works best for them, and they must contribute to the creation of their personalized curriculum. Today's educators can better harness the tools required to address a vibrant spectrum of learner differences and create profoundly dynamic educational experiences in their classrooms.

This is an updated version of an article published on the ISTE Blog on March 4, 2014.

Dale Basye is the author of the books Personalized Learning: A Guide for Engaging Students with Technology, Get Active: Reimagining Learning Spaces for Student Success and the Circles of Heck series for Random House Children's books. He's interested in creative ways of personalizing learning to meet the diverse needs of today's students to help them become better equipped to deal with the challenges of the digital age workplace.

30+ Tools for Diverse Learners

By Luis perez and Kendra Grant

New discoveries about the workings of the learning brain have converged with advancements in educational technology to finally make possible the kinds of flexible learning environments that students need to prepare for their future. According to the Universal Design for Learning (UDL) framework, flexibility is key because it allows educators to accommodate their students' natural variability in learning preferences.

The Center for Applied Specialized Technology (CAST) defines UDL as a framework to improve and optimize teaching and learning for all people based on scientific insights into how humans learn.

Neuroscience has revealed that learners show a great deal of variability in three key areas: in what they find motivating (the "why" of learning), in how they are able to take in and process information to make meaning from it (the "what" of learning) and in how they demonstrate their understanding (the "how" of learning).

Learners may be strong in one area (remembering the information they read) yet struggle and need support in the others (maintaining their focus or expressing their thoughts). Addressing this variability requires a more flexible approach to instruction that adapts the curriculum to the variable needs of learners, rather than the other way around.

To account for learner variability in each of these areas, CAST developed UDL guidelines that call on educators to provide options in the form of multiple means of engagement with learning, multiple means of representation for information and multiple means of action and expression through which learners can demonstrate their understanding.

The ultimate goal of these guidelines is to develop expert learners who are purposeful, motivated, resourceful, knowledgeable, strategic and goal directed. The goal of learner expertise ties directly into the ISTE Standards for Students, which empower students to take ownership of their learning as they build global competencies and develop deep thinking, collaboration and communication skills.

While UDL is first and foremost about implementing a flexible pedagogy, technology can help by making the kind of personalized learning envisioned under UDL a reality. Read on to find out about a number of free and low-cost UDL-aligned apps and websites that you can use to make learning environments more flexible and personalized. Or, if you prefer to view the list visually, take a look at our Pinterest board.

Tools for Engagement and the Affective Network

For students to be engaged, learning has to be relevant and meaningful on a personal level. Project-based learning (PBL) is one approach that achieves this goal by tying instruction to real-world concerns that really matter to learners.

With PBL, learners gain knowledge and skills as they investigate and respond to an authentic, engaging and complex problem or challenge over an extended period of time. In conducting their inquiry, learners may do online research as well as go out into their communities to gather information through surveys and interviews that place the problem in a more personally meaningful context.

As they learn about the problem in the context of their own communities, learners engage in ongoing reflection about not only their emerging understandings but also the process involved in their inquiry. At the conclusion of the project, they make their project work public, often by sharing it with a wider audience through a classroom website or blog.

A challenge of implementing PBL, however, is storing and organizing materials and resources so students can access them easily when they need them.

Here are a couple of our favorite cloud storage tools:

Google Drive. This web tool/mobile app provides an easily accessible collaborative environment where students can create and share information related to their PBL activities. Drive supports the creation of documents, spreadsheets, presentations, drawings and forms (for data collection) that are stored online, always backed up and accessible from any web browser or through dedicated apps on iOS and Android devices. Learners can collaborate on these documents in real time and even chat with each other as they brainstorm ideas and make changes to the content.

Dropbox. This online file storage app, similar to Google Drive, allows students to store documents and access them from any device while working on collaborative projects.

Here are some of the best student-response tools:

Nearpod. This app allows the teacher to broadcast a presentation with embedded polls and quizzes. You can control the pace of the presentation, and as learners respond from their devices, you can see the results in real time and adjust the lesson accordingly.

Peardeck. This tool works in a similar way. Learners can follow along with the teacher's presentation and answer interactive questions from any device that can connect to the internet.

Socrative. This tool lets you create quick assessments on any web-enabled device. Unlike Nearpod, Socrative does not have a presentation component.

Plickers. This system is unique in that it doesn't require learners to have devices to respond. They just hold up a card with a special code that can be read by an app on the teacher's device to collect the responses.

Tools for Representation and the Recognition Network

For much of the history of education, print has been the primary way students have received information. If a learner could not process that type of information well, he or she was labeled disabled. The digital revolution, however, has created new options for presenting information in a multitude of formats to accommodate the many different ways learners prefer to retrieve and process information.

On both iOS and Android devices, a number of built-in accessibility options make it possible for the learner to customize the size of the text, invert the display for better contrast and make other adjustments to the display of text and the interface.

Check out these tools that make it easier to read on the web:

Safari Reader. This built-in option of the Safari web browser on Macs and iOS devices allows learners to remove the navigation, ads and other visual clutter from a web page to better focus on the content. Safari Reader has options for customizing the text size, the background color and the font for a customized reading experience. With iOS 11 and Mac OS High Sierra, learners can even set up Safari Reader to automatically activate on web pages that support this feature.

Mercury Reader, Just Read and Easy Reader. The Chrome web browser does not have a native option for removing the clutter from web pages, but learners can choose from a variety of free extensions that perform a similar function:

OneNote Web Clipper. Learners can use the free Web Clipper to save articles to their OneNote account for access from any device that supports that service. Once the article is in OneNote, learners can activate the Immersive Reader feature to view a clutter-free version of the article and use text-to-speech to listen to it as they follow along with the word highlighting. Immersive Reader is highly customizable and includes a number of display themes as well as options for adjusting the text size and line spacing, displaying the parts of speech and more.

While some learners may need to customize only the display of the information, others may need to have the information presented in a different format to account for limitations in their sight or hearing. Fortunately, accessibility is now a built-in option on major operating systems.

For learners who have trouble reading on screens, try these basic screen-reading tools:

VoiceOver. This is the built-in screen reader for iOS. It uses synthesized speech or braille (with a connected braille display) to describe what is on the screen to someone who is blind.

TalkBack. The built-in screen reader for Android devices, TalkBack is similar to VoiceOver but does not include braille support out of the box. However, it does support it when you install a separate component called BrailleBack.

ChromeVox. You can use this free screen reader, which is available on Chromebooks and as an extension to the Chrome web browser, to provide better access to content for students who are blind or who have low vision. It is also helpful for a variety of other learners, including those who struggle with decoding and those who prefer to listen to audio.

Here are the go-to text-to-speech tools:

Speak Selection and Speak Screen. These two iOS built-in text-to-speech features include word and sentence highlighting and the kind of high-quality voice that used to be available only on the Mac. With Speak Screen, a special gesture (swiping from the top of the screen with two fingers) will activate an automatic reading move that will also flip the pages of an electronic book or scroll a long web page. Speak Screen also shows on-screen controls for adjusting the speaking rate.

Voice Dream Reader. This full-featured document manager expands on the capabilities of the built-in text-to-speech with even more options for personalization, including fully customizable colors for the word and sentence highlighting, masking to display only a few lines of text at a time, support for dyslexia-friendly fonts and more. Documents can be imported from a number of sources such as Google Drive, Dropbox and Bookshare, a service that provides free access to books in accessible formats for students with qualifying print disabilities ($14.99 for iOS, $9.99 for Android).

Announcify. This free Chrome extension can also read a web page aloud. While it does not provide word highlighting, it blurs out most of the page and shows only a small section in focus to direct attention.

TextHelp Read&Write. This Chrome extension provides a number of UDL supports for language and symbols, including text-to-speech, translation, a picture dictionary and highlighting. The free extension is available to any educator with a valid school email address, and a fully functional 30-day trial gives everyone access to the text-to-speech features even after the trial ends.

Quillsoft WordQ for Chrome. This app offers an easy-to-use writing space (compatible with Google Docs) for Chromebooks that includes word prediction, speech feedback and Google Voice Typing. WordQ's word prediction features also work offline, a boon for schools and students with spotty or limited access to the internet. The app's perpetual license is transferable and eliminates yearly renewal costs.

Once learners have access to the information, the next step is to help them make sense of it. One way teachers can help students make sense of vast amounts of information is by highlighting some of the key patterns, concepts and relationships — in other words, the big ideas.

Here are some tools that use visual strategies to help students make sense of ideas:

Inspiration. Inspiration is a powerful visual mapping tool with an integrated linear outline. Learners use the diagram view to visually brainstorm, plan and organize their ideas using color, shapes and images. Learners can quickly create detailed concept maps and graphic organizers, moving to the outline view when they are ready to expand upon their ideas in writing. Any changes in one view are captured in the other. Learners can easily switch between the diagram and outline view to meet their needs and preferences. There is a desktop version (Inspiration), iOS apps (Inspiration Maps and Kidspiration Maps, $9.99) as well as an online version (Webspiration).

Popplet. This tool available on the web and as an iOS app makes it easy to build simple concept maps, which is a great way to activate a learner's prior knowledge. Ask them to create a concept map at the beginning of a lesson, then have them make a new one at the end of the unit that builds on their first map. Popplet has a free "Lite" version for test driving the app with only one concept map. It costs $4.99.

Tools for Action, Expression and the Strategic Network

Just as print was the primary way learners accessed information in the past, so writing has been the main way students demonstrate their understanding. Unfortunately, this puts some learners at a disadvantage, including those whose motor challenges make it difficult to hold a pencil, type or use a mouse, or those with processing or memory issues.

Dictation is a built-in feature on iOS devices for students who would rather speak their answers instead of entering text with an onscreen keyboard. No prior training is necessary for the speech recognition to work, but an internet connection is required. The speech recognition features built into both Windows and Mac provide support for a number of commands that perform common tasks, including opening applications and entering and formatting text. The enhanced dictation feature on the Mac even lets you create new custom commands.

Students who struggle with traditional means of expression, such as writing a paper, can also use video or audio to show their understanding in a variety of creative ways.

Some of our favorite video and screencasting tools include:

Clips. As the name implies, this free iOS app from Apple is meant for creating short videos that can be more easily shared through social media and messaging services. A standout feature of Clips is the ability to automatically add subtitles to the videos it creates to make them more accessible.

iMovie. Students who are ready to step up from Clips can use the free iMovie for iOS app to shoot and edit a documentary or short film that captures key ideas about a topic with video clips, photos, music and audio narration. For those who need a more powerful editor, the Mac version of iMovie (also free) is an even better option.

TouchCast Studio. This free iPad app has everything learners need to create interactive videos that include hotspots linking to a variety of web content. Learners can use a number of video apps (vApps) to link to supporting research on the web, ask questions through polls, link to a script of their video for accessibility and more. The app has a number of advanced features, including a built-in teleprompter, green screen capabilities to allow learners to place themselves into different settings and multi-camera support through a connected iPhone.

Story Remix. This is the follow-up to the popular but now discontinued Windows Movie Maker (available for free with the Windows 10 Fall Creators Update). Learners can combine photos, video clips, music and audio narration to tell a story. Remix can even automatically generate a video by selecting the best shots and clips. Learners can use the video as is, or further customize it with a number of effects that include 3D objects and animated characters. Learners who need a more powerful video editor can look to commercial options such as Adobe Premiere Elements ($99.99) or Pinnacle Studio (starting at $59).

WeVideo. Chromebook users have fewer options for video due to the limited hardware built into their devices, but they can perform basic edits with this Chrome app. WeVideo is available with a number of subscription plans (depending on the features and storage space needed) that start at $4.99 per month for individuals (with volume pricing for schools).

In lieu of full video, students can use these audio-only tools instead:

GarageBand. This free app for iOS devices makes it easy for students to capture and edit audio and to create podcasts and other audio recordings that summarize their understanding at the end of a lesson. It's also great for audio reflections.

Audacity. This free and popular cross-platform tool provides basic recording and editing functions, but students will need to find royalty-free loops on sites such as incompetech if they want to add a music soundtrack.

Before learners can creatively express their understanding in a variety of ways, they need to organize their thoughts and come up with a good plan. A number of tools allow learners to practice, refine and augment this set of skills, which fall under the umbrella of executive functioning.

These note-taking apps, for instance, allow them to easily capture and organize information in a variety of formats:

Google Keep. This free tool lets students store notes online so they can access them from any device with an internet connection, and it gives them multiple ways to save information, including taking photos, typing it in or recording it with their voice.

Notability. This iOS app records audio while learners take notes via text, photos, web links and handwriting. The notes are synchronized to the audio so learners can quickly find a specific point in the recording by tapping in the corresponding section of the notes ($9.99).

Book Creator. Book Creator provides a blank canvas where learners can bring together all of their media to demonstrate their understanding by publishing an ePub ebook. Each book can include text, images (with descriptions for assistive technologies), audio and video. The fully functional free version of Book Creator for the iPad can be used to create a single book. Upgrading to the paid ($4.99) version not only unlocks unlimited publishing, it also adds some comic book templates. A web version of Book Creator that works on Chromebooks is also available. Teachers can create up to 40 books for free with that version.

Just as a carpenter has a toolbelt with a number of options to choose from to best suit the nature of each job, so technology gives educators a wide array of options for engaging learners and helping them access their learning environment. The key to taking best advantage of these new tools is to think pedagogy first, technology second. In other words, don't make adopting the technology a goal unto itself, but rather select the tool based on how well it fits the particular learning goals of your unit or lesson.

When used in a thoughtful way, technology opens up many possibilities for learners to find and develop their own voices, take ownership of their learning and become creators of knowledge instead of just consumers of information.

This is an updated version of an article the was published on the ISTE Blog on June 8, 2015.

Luis Pérez is a senior technical assistance specialist for the National Accessible Educational Materials for Learning Center at CAST. He holds a doctorate in special education and a master's in instructional technology from the University of South Florida.

Kendra Grant's multifaceted career includes stints as a teacher, library media specialist, special ed coordinator, co-founder of a professional learning company, online course creator and large-scale technology implementation consultant. She holds a masters of educational technology from the University of British Columbia.

Turn Your Classroom into a Personalized Learning Environment

By Robyn Howton

By now you've probably heard of personalized learning, which tailors instruction, expression of learning and assessment to each student's unique needs and preferences. While one-on-one instruction geared toward the strengths and challenges of each student has always been an ideal, only in recent years have technological advances allowed it to become a reality in public education.

Personalized learning capitalizes on students' almost instinctual ability to use technology, but it is so much more than technology and algorithms. It is the purposeful design of blended instruction to combine face-to-face teaching, technology-assisted instruction and student-to-student collaboration to leverage each student's learning preferences and interests for deeper learning. When done right, it meets several of the ISTE Standards for Students and ISTE Standards for Educators while leading to a more rigorous, challenging, engaging and thought-provoking curriculum.

Over the last four years, I have transformed my traditional classroom into a blended-learning environment that provides a more personalized learning experience for each one of my students. It hasn't been easy. It's taken a lot of research, trial and error, and adjustments. But the results have definitely been worth it.

Here are five lessons I've learned that have helped me take my classroom from a traditional sage-on-the-stage affair to a tech-assisted personalized learning haven.

1. Learn from Others

I won't lie. The journey from old school to new learning paradigm was bumpy at first. I tried blended lessons that took less time than planned, had technology failures, chose the wrong method of delivery for various types of content or skills, and generally made every mistake you can imagine. But I didn't give up, and eventually I had more successes than failures. My students' input and further pedagogical study helped me refine my lesson planning until I got it right.

I started by researching personalized and blended learning as a member of the Rodel Teacher Council (RTC) to create the Blueprint for Personalized Learning in Delaware. I was also a member of the BRINC Consortium, a group formed to implement blended learning in several Delaware districts.

Being able to work with other teachers also implementing blended learning was key to my continued growth. We worked with Modern Teacher to understand the shifts in pedagogy necessary to transition to blended learning. I heard Caitlin Tucker at a BRINC training and have used her books to guide my continued development.

All of these experiences helped me find more effective ways to lead my students while empowering them to take responsibility for their own learning. On top of that, learning from and collaborating with others is a hallmark of the new ISTE Standards for Educators, which advise us to "dedicate time to collaborate with both colleagues and students to improve practice, discover and share resources and ideas, and solve problems."

2. Use the Technology You Have

Although it is not the focus of a student-centered classroom, technology plays a big part in the success of this approach because it allows the differentiation of instruction, assessment and expression of learning as well as the collection of student data.

We don't have a 1:1 environment at this time, but the students — who are my co-learners and teachers — have helped me adapt to whatever tools are available. The standard hardware in core content classrooms throughout my district includes a set of 15 iPads, a projector and a document camera.

Students are allowed to use their cell phones for educational purposes. We use Schoology as a learning management system. I use Google Classroom and curriculum sites, such as CommonLit | Free Fiction & Nonfiction Literacy Resources, to embed high-quality digital content within our LMS. Much to my surprise, technology itself plays the smallest role in providing personalized learning for my students.

3. Let Students Make Choices

When I first embarked on this mission, I decided to "release" one piece of the assignment at a time in an effort to control students' pathway through the material. Since then, I have learned to take a more personalized approach to assignments, which also aligns to the ISTE Standard for Educators that advise us to "foster a culture where students take ownership of their learning goals and outcomes in both independent and group settings."

Class often starts with a mini-lesson, which then flows into students making choices about what they need to do next to meet specific learning targets aligned to the standards.

My units in Schoology offer guidance to the students while allowing them to choose their own learning pathways and complete the activities in the order that makes the most sense to them.

For instance, while reading a short story, they can choose between just reading or reading along as they listen to a story. They can also decide whether to annotate online or on a printed copy. They can take notes on paper or record their thoughts verbally as they analyze the story.

While my students are still required to write traditional essays on many assignments, they also get the chance to show their learning in a variety of other ways. When appropriate, they can submit their analysis by writing a traditional essay, creating a website, creating infographics, writing a script for a video that they then record or via a communication tool they suggest.

4. Choose the Best Content Delivery Method

I had another a-ha moment when I finally understood how to choose the right delivery method for various types of content. My first few attempts included finding a video on each topic to provide background information or delivering a face-to-face lecture on a new concept, followed by an online quiz. My inaugural online lesson consisted of a folder with a page for my essential question, a copy of my PowerPoint and a link for students to submit their notes.

But I was simply using technology in place of my normal face-to-face teaching. When asked to explain the "why" behind my choices during professional learning sessions, I realized there was more to creating blended lessons than simply adding technology.

Today, I carefully construct my units with specific learning goals that drive the method of delivery and learning activities. When deciding how to structure my lessons, I look at the learning activities I've used in the past to decide which were successful and which need to be refined or replaced. As a result, instead of lecturing to students and showing them a PowerPoint during class time, I often give them screencasts or videos to watch at home.

The screencasts, which I create with Zaption, Screencast-O-Matic and VideoAnt, are better than PowerPoints because students can hear my voice instead of clicking through a silent slide deck. And videos are better than face-to-face lectures because they can skip forward, pause or rewind as needed until they get the lesson. They still get a chance to ask questions during our class time or online.

This flipped learning setup frees up my students to use class time to practice their skills. For instance, they might annotate a short story or poem in Google Docs or take part in a Socratic seminar. During our unit on research into social justice issues, students receive a digital review of the research process and choose their learning activities based on their needs. Some may meet with me to review how to embed quotes while other groups start planning their presentations and still others work independently on gathering valid research.

5. Assess as You Go

Instead of just giving a final exam at the end of each unit, I try to use formative assessment to enable me to give my students guidance and assistance when they need it. I use a variety of methods for this. For instance, my video lectures often include interactive questions to assess their understanding of the material. Playposit and TED-Ed: Lessons Worth Sharing are my go-to tools for this type of assessment. And our classroom is often noisy and active as we play a round of Kahoot, which gives me instant, actionable feedback on what we need to do next, who needs to be pulled into a small group for reteaching and who would be better off in a group that pursues extended learning while I reteach the rest of the class.

I also gather formative assessment data through:

- Discussion threads.

- Self-grading quizzes that give students immediate and actionable feedback on their proficiency in specific skills.

- Monitoring of students works in progress on Google Docs.

- Exit tickets, which assess the class' comfort level with new concepts.

I use all of this data to inform adjustments to learning activities as well as selection of resources to help students meet the standards addressed in the unit. When the assessments show a student has mastered a skill, I can provide them with instruction to go deeper or learn new skills.

6. Pull It all Together

My original objective was to transform my classroom into a blended learning model that would give my students the best access to rigorous, engaging, personalized learning experiences.

Going into my fifth year, I am pleased with the progress we've made toward this goal and excited to implement new ideas including more flexibility in seating and groups as well as a better use of formative data.

My classroom today is a vastly different place than it was five years ago. Instead of showing up to class to hear me deliver all the content and teach the skills they need to meet the standards for our curriculum, my students are now the masters of their own learning destinies.

Instead of relying on notes they take during one-time lectures, they can access and even return to my videos and screencasts and other resources when they need them most, as they are working on an assignment or reviewing for a test.

My role used to be standing in front of the room lecturing about the research process, modeling various components and monitoring students' progress toward a final, correctly formatted research paper.

Recently, I began partnering with the Human Ecology Foundation to expose my students to a range of real-world issues. The students then form groups and choose one to research and propose a solution or way to make an impact. Not only are they learning to do authentic research, they will be volunteering and learning about the issue through firsthand experience. Students can even win a scholarship for their research and projects!

I am available to assist students, conduct check-ins and assess their individual responsibilities and group outcomes throughout the project. But most of the time I just stay out of the way while they learn how to effectively research, collaborate and create presentations together.

The biggest compliment I have received since all this started came from a student in my AP Language and Composition class. He told me, "Your class is easy. I don't mean simple — I mean it is easy for me to learn because I can pick assignments that let me do my best work."

I strive to make my classes that kind of "easy" for every student I teach. Across the board, my students acknowledge that they feel better prepared for college or jobs because of our use of collaborative technology. I've had students who are now in college tell me that our use of digital content made it easier for them to adjust to college.

This is an updated version of an article posted on the ISTE Blog on May 19, 2015.

Robyn Howton is English department chair and the AVID (Advancement Via Individual Determination) coordinator at Mount Pleasant High School in Wilmington, Delaware. She is a member of the Rodel Teacher Council, which created the Blueprint for Personalized Learning in Delaware, and a member of the original cohort of the BRINC consortium.

Schools Have No Choice but to Personalize Learning

By Nancy Weinstein

Personalized learning in schools is no longer a choice, but a necessity. After all, students are already personalizing their own learning. According to Common Sense Media, teens spend most of their time outside of school consuming media.

In those hours, they choose what they will learn, how they will learn and from whom they will learn.

It shouldn't be surprising, then, that the latest Gallup study shows that most students are disengaged in classrooms where educators prescribe what they will learn, when they will learn it and how they will demonstrate their learning.

While the Gallup study does not directly show causation between the increase in media consumption with the decline in student engagement, the study authors specifically cite the "lack of experiential and project-based learning pathways for students" as one of three primary sources of failure (The other two sources, an overemphasis on standardized testing and lack of non-college pathways, fail to explain why the highest academic performers are disengaged along with the non-college bound).

If we want to re-energize and re-engage our students, we have no choice but to give them opportunities to choose what they will learn and how they learn it. It's no wonder the ISTE Standards for Students define Standard 1, Empowered Learner, as someone who "leverages technology to take an active role in choosing, achieving and demonstrating competency in her learning goals."

While there is no single proven model to personalize instruction, we do know that technology, when merged with good pedagogy offers the most efficient and effective solutions. Amazing progress is already happening at institutions like AltSchools, Buck Institute for Education, New Classrooms and The Learning Accelerator.

If you're at a school that is still not ready to make the transition, your students do not, and should not, need to wait. There are ways for teachers to personalize instruction within the existing curriculum. Consider these ideas:

1. Allow students to select from multiple options for practicing skills. Students do not need to memorize math facts, vocabulary or spelling words the same way. Some might still choose worksheets or paper flashcards. Others can pick from digital options like TenMarks, IXL or Bitsboard. Giving students choice will increase motivation. Teachers can and should still guide students based on their level of mastery, speed and how they best take feedback.

2. Let students choose how to demonstrate mastery. A written paper is one way to demonstrate understanding of a topic, but there are many others. Besides, it's an essential life skill to present in multiple formats. Allow students to use sites such as Haiku Deck or Show Me for engaging digital presentations. Have reluctant writers in the room? Consider letting them make a digital comic with a site like Pixton. For a change of pace, try International Literary Association's Trading Cards app to create virtual trading cards of historical figures or book characters.

3. Give students a broader audience. Students are often warned that anything they post online can be seen and shared by people outside their intended audience. Why not give them the opportunity to learn digital citizenship skills and encourage them to share their work with a broad audience. The ISTE Standards for Students define their second standard, Digital Citizen, as someone who "recognizes the rights, responsibilities and opportunities of living, learning and working in an interconnected digital world, and they act and model in ways that are safe, legal and ethical."

But those skills must be practiced to be learned. Younger students can use restricted sites like EasyBlogJr, and older students can try safe sites like Teen Ink, Write the World and Figment. When students post for an audience, they are likely to feel a greater sense of purpose and care more about the quality of their work. They will also learn from reading and critiquing the work of their peers worldwide. And if issues do arise — like inappropriate or offensive comments — it's an opportunity to teach them in the moment.

We will only stem what Gallup describes as our monumental, collective national failure to engage our students when everyone accepts that personalized learning in schools is not a fad. There is absolutely no way that the genie is going back in the bottle, and we shouldn't want it to. We should embrace the use of technology to make learning magical for each and every student.

This is an updated version of an article posted on the ISTE Blog on August 24, 2016.

Nancy Weinstein is the founder and CEO of Mindprint Learning, a smart assessment solution for understanding student's non-academic strengths and needs. She has an MBA from Harvard Business School and a BSE in bioengineering from the University of Pennsylvania. Weinstein is the author of the forthcoming workbook "A Classroom Guide to Self-Regulated Learning" from CAST-UDL Publishing.

Video: Personalize Learning and Empower Students to Change Their Stories

In this compelling video, teacher Katharine Hale explains that the way educators employ edtech in schools can be a story-changer or a story-repeater for students.

In this Ignite talk from ISTE 2016, Hale challenges you to take on what she calls "the single story problem" in schools. Traditionally, education has reinforced a single idea of want academic success looks like and, for kids who don't fit the mold, their stories go like this: average student, special ed, behavior problem.

Hale urges teachers to integrate tech thoughtfully and meaningfully to personalize learning and help students write their own stories.

Watch the video at **www.youtube.com/watch?v=tHQ_smL5g6k&t=5s**

Resources

For more on personalized learning, check out these ISTE resources.

Personalized Learning: A Guide for Engaging Students with Technology by Peggy Grant and Dale Basye. ISTE members get 25% off at iste.org/PersonalizedLearning.

Learning Supercharged: Digital Age Strategies and Insights from the EdTech Frontier by Lynne Schrum with Sandi Sumerfield. ISTE members get 25% off at iste.org/LearningSupercharged.

4

Digital Citizenship

In This Chapter:

Living and working in the digital age demands that all students act and model in ways that are safe, legal and ethical. But these days, digital citizenship is so much more than what not to do. Students need to feel empowered to create, share, solve, collaborate and connect with others in their classrooms and across the world. The new digital citizenship is all about being an empowered learner.

The selections in this chapter will help you understand what the new digital citizenship looks like in practice as you teach, mentor and guide empowered learners.

Proactive Not Protective: Digital Citizenship Should Empower Students

By Sarah Stoeckl

Digital citizenship is one of the hottest topics in education today. As technology has proliferated in schools and beyond, questions about the correct ways to use that technology have likewise cropped up like dandelions. Frequently, these questions arise in response to perceived dangers or misbehaviors — identity theft, adult predators, cyberbullying, illegal actions — and so the education around digital citizenship often appears like a list of rules and regulations: Shut it down. Lock it up. Don't do that. Be afraid.

The ISTE Standards for Students represent a shift in this perspective, a drive to reformulate our approach to digital citizenship in education. With the standards' overarching focus on learner empowerment, students are expected to thoughtfully lead their own learning, and educators are thus pushed to support and facilitate them in this goal. This empowered approach applies to digital citizenship as well.

The Digital Citizen standard brings this empowerment to how students interact online. First off, it calls for students to drive their digital citizenship as they "recognize the rights, responsibilities and opportunities of living, learning and working in an interconnected digital world, and they act and model in ways that are safe, legal and ethical." The statement highlights not only the responsibilities of interactions online but also the rights that students have as global and national citizens, the opportunities the internet facilitates, and students' ability to model safe, legal and ethical behaviors for others. From the get-go, the focus is on complexity and proactive behavior, rather than fears and regulations.

Here are a few ways we might see this shift in practice:

- Teach students about intellectual property and the legal and ethical ramifications of misusing others' work while simultaneously teaching Creative Commons and proper citation guidelines and tools. Empower students to share and protect their own work when, where and to what extent they choose.

- Help students collaboratively learn about and discuss online tracking of personal data, the limitations of privacy settings on digital products and services, and the way that algorithms curate information for users based on past behaviors. They then reflect individually and make changes they feel comfortable with to their privacy settings and online behavior.

- Encourage students to interact on the internet with an eye to its potential power in terms of self-representation, collaboration with others around the world, entrepreneurialism, activism and engagement, and creativity and sharing.

The best way to meet this vision for dynamic, ethical and responsible behavior online is by knitting digital citizenship instruction throughout the curriculum and student learning activities. It also comes when educators recognize openings in the course of learning to call out knowledge, pitfalls and opportunities related to digital activity. By approaching digital citizenship more holistically, and as a series of learner-driven activities and mindsets, we foster engaged citizens — whenever and wherever our students interact.

This is an updated version of an article published on the ISTE Blog on March 29, 2017.

Sarah Stoeckl, Ph.D., is ISTE's senior project manager in the Standards Department. Her work focuses on the refresh of the ISTE Standards and implementation of the standards in education.

The New Digital Citizenship: Empower Proactive Digital Learners

As digital agents, students leverage technology to help solve the world's problems, advocate for equal rights and digital access for everyone and influence societal norms.

Digital interactors communicate with empathy and authenticity, collaborate with others online to accomplish goals and apply critical thinking to all online sources.

Finally, students must cultivate a digital self by proactively managing their digital identity and privacy, respecting the privacy and rights of others and understanding the permanence of the digital world.

Watch the animation at the following link to dive into the new digital citizenship, then share it with students, colleagues, administrators, parents and community members. It's time to come together and empower students to cultivate digital citizenship at home, at school and everywhere in between.

https://youtu.be/NOYu35BbMNU

Webinar: Bringing Digital Citizenship to Life

Most digital citizenship lessons are centered on students' relationships with their devices, or, in other words, what not to do! While it's imperative that students understand how to manage safety and privacy as well as understand how to be nice online, there is so much more to digital citizenship.

In this hour-long webinar recording, find out from Kristen Mattson. Ed.D., and Jamie Lewsadder what it means for students to be participatory digital citizens. The webinar is packed with exciting classroom lesson and project ideas that empower students and allow them to practice digital citizenship skills in real-world environments.

Visit this link to get started: **http://iste.adobeconnect.com/ptfnpwknn04c/** (You must download Adobe Connect to view the recording).

Find Free and Fair Use Photos

By Keith Ferrell

Grabbing images from Google is easy. You search, copy and paste. It's a no-brainer and often the first thing students do when creating any sort of digital project that requires images.

But how do your students know if they have permission to use someone else's photos? To be in alignment with the ISTE Standards for Students on digital citizenship, students need to understand copyright and how to find royalty-free images that are OK to use in projects.

One example of a digital activity that requires royalty-free media is a book trailer project I often assign to my fifth graders. Students create 60- to 90-second movie trailers of books they have read. The trailer consists of a series of images and text that work together to tell the story of the book that excites readers without giving away too much of the plot. The trailer is coupled with a royalty-free soundtrack (we use Soundzabound) to add to the drama and auditory aesthetics of the final product.

The images they use must also be royalty-free and fair use.

Here are four great sites I've found to search for royalty-free photos. These resources can help students learn at an early age the idea of copyright. Giving students the knowledge and tools to make decisions about their work is a key component of empowering learners.

> **Pics4Learning.** This site offers a safe, free image library for education. Teachers and students can use the copyright-friendly photos and images for classrooms, multimedia projects, websites, videos, portfolios or any other project in an educational setting. It's easy to use, and all of the copyright information is available in a simplistic bibliography underneath any chosen photo.
>
> **flickrCC.** This is a good place to start when looking for Creative Commons images. The panel on the left displays a collage of the first 36 photos matching your search term. Click on any of these thumbnails to get a slightly larger image and the attribution details displayed on the

right. Right-click the image and choose a size. Most photos have small, medium and large sizes. Next, hit "save image as" and save it in a folder. Above the photo, you'll find attribution text that must be included with any work you produce using the picture.

Photos for Class. This is similar to Pics4Learning. You simply run a search, click on a thumbnail and the photo downloads with the copyright information as a caption on the photo.

If it seems like finding royalty-free images is an extra step, just remember: As our students' lives and school work move more into the digital realm, it's important that we, as educators, lead by example and show the ethical and appropriate ways to cite work and give credit where credit is due.

This is an updated version of an article published on the ISTE Blog on Nov. 15, 2017.

Keith Farrell is an educational technology coach at Singapore American School. He's taught internationally since 2001 and has worked as a technology coordinator, integration specialist, classroom teacher and coach. He blogs at edtechideas.com. Follow him on Twitter @k_ferrell.

Don't Ban Social Media — Teach Students How to Be Digital Citizens

By Nikki D Robertson

Alarming headlines about social media can leave the impression there's an evil monster eagerly waiting to steal away our innocent children and devour them one click at a time.

While some of the fears about social media and our students are certainly valid, the response of some school officials and parents to ban, forbid and restrict can be short-sighted. By taking away social media, schools and parents believe they are keeping their children safe from cyberbullies, sexual predators and other online threats.

This approach, however, not only leaves our children ill-prepared to safely and knowledgeably deal with the dangers social media can present, it also fails to teach them how to be good digital citizens and successfully harness the power of social media as an important tool for learning.

Don't Just Tell, Show!

Walking hand-in-hand to various places with my granddaughter recently, I talked to her about and modeled safety rules for crossing the road. We put our hand up above our eyes in a searching stance. I said out loud and mimicked with exaggerated motions, "We look both ways before we cross the road. Look to the left. Look to the right. All clear? If yes, let's go. If no, wait. Always be safe."

After she went through these steps in a real situation, I asked her if it was safe to cross the road. If she had learned to cross the road safely by talking about it, reading about it, coloring a picture illustrating it, watching a video about it or playing a video game focused on it, I would have been uneasy sending her out into the world to navigate the roads.

As parents, grandparents and educators, part of our job is to teach and model how to safely navigate the physical world. We don't lock our children in the house until they are legal adults and then scoot them out the door, hoping the life lessons we taught through various simulations will transfer to real-life experiences.

Let Students Practice

Similarly, while we can "lock" students out of social media and attempt to teach them how to navigate the virtual world through songs, color sheets, books, videos, online programs or game simulations, nothing leaves a deeper impact on students than actually allowing students to see proper social media usage modeled daily by respected adults (parents, teachers, administrators) and by allowing students to use social media properly in the actual space.

Here are some ways to model positive social media use:

>   **Connect with experts.** Use social media to connect with authors, in-the-field experts and other schools to demonstrate the power of connecting and learning together.

Let student take over. Allow students to "take over" the classroom social media account. Allow students to take pictures and video of activities that get them excited about learning. Students can start doing this as early as kindergarten using a school or classroom social media account. Be sure to set clear rules for student take-over time, including getting permission from those who will be in your pictures and videos, teaching them how to compose a social media post and running the post past the teacher before posting to social media.

Engage in real conversations. Use student social media "mistakes" as opportunities to teach, not punish. I learned this valuable lesson from my former assistant principals, Jennifer Hogan and Holly Sutherland. Not only did these two brilliant educators and founders of #ALEdChat and #USEdChat model social media use as an important and valuable education tool, they also gently monitored student social media use.

When a student inevitably used social media in a less-than-desirable way, they would take the opportunity to discuss, not admonish, their decision-making process for what was posted. This allowed students to "fail" within the safe confines of school and learn from their mistakes before similar mistakes as adults could have lifelong consequences.

Modeling use of social media through authentic, real-life situations is the best way to ensure our students will not only know how to use social media responsibly, but will also understand why doing so is important.

Nikki D Robertson is author of the book, *Connected Librarians: Tap Social Media to Enhance Professional Development and Student Learning*. She's also a veteran educator, school librarian, instructional technology facilitator and a member of the ISTE Librarians Network.

A New Twist on Cyberbullying

By Cynde Reneau

Over the years, I've worked hard to teach my students about appropriate online behavior. I've spent a lot of time teaching students to "do this" or "don't do that" online. While I feel this method works for younger students, I've come to realize that high school students require a different approach. Older students don't respond well to lecturing and finger-pointing. For something to stick, they need to draw their own conclusions. Therefore, we need to guide them, not preach to them.

That's easier said than done. Finding new tactics for teaching digital citizenship is difficult because most educator resources don't stray far from the traditional "Thou shalt not" approach. That's what prompted me to look for my own resources. In doing so, I came up with a three-pronged approach that engages my students in discussions about digital citizenship rather than patronizing them.

Teach Consequences

After seeing firsthand a few students lose college scholarships due to senseless mistakes on social media, I decided to look for videos or materials that would focus on what happens if students don't stop and think about what they do online. I found just what I was looking for at Netsmartz Workshop, a program created by the National Center for Missing & Exploited Children, which provides age-appropriate resources for teaching students how to be safe on and offline.

The video, called "2 Kinds of Stupid," perfectly illustrates the consequences of posting inappropriate content online.

The three-minute animation tells the tale of Edvardo, a good student and champion swimmer who's primed to win a college athletic scholarship — until he takes selfies of himself drinking at a party and posts them on Facebook. He doesn't make his pictures "private," so everyone can see them, including his coach, teammates, parents and principal.

Ultimately, the consequences are stiff. He gets kicked off the swim team and suspended from school, and he loses any chance of earning a college scholarship. My students, who are competitive by nature and want to be successful, could identify with the student who made bad choices and paid a very high price.

Teach Empathy

The next step is to tap into students' natural empathy. Again, I like to share scenarios that my students can relate to. I start by telling the story of two best friends who unwittingly find themselves in a cyberbullying predicament. One girl buys a new swimming suit and posts a picture on social media of herself wearing it. The suit is unflattering and not a good fit, so the best friend posts under the picture, "Did you check the size?" Numerous mean-spirited comments follow. The best friend feels awful because she didn't mean for her comment to spur such a humiliating response.

After asking students what the friend could have done differently, hands shot into the air from students eager to offer solutions. One student felt the girl who inadvertently wrote the hurtful comment should pick up the phone and call her friend to apologize. Another student suggested that someone post a nice comment, and another said someone should stand up for the girl.

That prompted a lengthy discussion. When you feel that pang of empathy, do you stick up for the student being bullied, ignore it or join in?

Using a literary reference that I knew students would appreciate, I reminded them of a well-known quote in the book Harry Potter and the Sorcerer's Stone. After the character Neville tries to stop his friends from doing something undoubtedly dangerous, Hogwarts headmaster Albus Dumbledore acknowledges Neville's act of courage when he says, "It takes a great deal of bravery to stand up to our enemies, but just as much to stand up to our friends."

Teaching Identity Strength

Let's face it: Cyberbullying is serious and it's happening every day in our schools. But when adults constantly toss out slogans like "Be a buddy, not a bully," or post signs designating "Bully-free zones," the words begin to lose their impact. Just as in the 1970s, when anti-drug campaigns were scoffed at by the very people they were targeting, anti-bullying campaigns are also losing their effectiveness.

I got a taste of this firsthand when I spoke to students about sexting, online safety and cyberbullying at an all-school assembly. When a student blurted out an obscenity during the sexting portion, the students went wild and didn't listen to a thing I said. I was frustrated and discouraged.

Later, I offered to award an iPad mini to the student who produced the best video and poster. Even that got little response.

The fact is, anti-bullying clichés have become a shut-off switch. What we really need to be doing is giving students actual skills to prevent bullying. To get that conversation going, I pose this question to students: "Will you accept the identity that others give you?"

Few students have thought of the problem this way before. Allowing them to discuss their vision for life and empowering them to reject the vision others try to give them is key. It's important to talk about someone they can relate to who had a vision and was successful. For this, I talk about Steve Jobs and how he never let anyone interfere with his vision for technology. Lady Gaga has also spoken pointedly about being bullied in school by kids who called her "ugly" and laughed at the way she dressed and sang. But she followed her vision to stardom.

Give Students a Voice

Allowing students to be involved in the conversation is the most important part of digital citizenship education. You can do this by posing questions in a class discussion or, to encourage more frank conversation, you can use online interactive polling software, such as Socrative or Poll Everywhere.

I did this by asking students at an assembly to get on their devices to answer some questions, while stressing that their answers would absolutely be anonymous. Then I asked questions like:

- Have you ever done something inappropriate online?
- Do you know someone who's done something inappropriate online?
- Have you been bullied online?

More than 90 percent of the students participating in the assembly answered the poll questions. As I showed the results, students shouted questions like, "What do you mean by inappropriate?" "How can you tell someone anonymously if you know someone is being bullied?"

Students were engaged and eager to talk, and the discussion was frank and educational — for both students and staff. No shame, no finger-pointing, no condescending admonishments. These students are about to go out into the world, it's important that we not just educate them academically but prepare them for their lives.

This is an updated version of an article that was published on the ISTE Blog on Oct. 23, 2014.

Cynde Reneau is director of technology and innovation at Leman International School in Chengdu, China. She has been involved with technology integration for over 20 years. She is an ISTE presenter, an Apple Certified Trainer and a Google Certified Educator.

Resources

For further reading on digital citizenship, check out these ISTE resources.

Digital Citizenship in Action: Empowering Students to Engage in Online Communities, by Kristen Mattson. ISTE members save 25% at iste.org/DigCitAction.

Digital Citizenship in Schools, Third Edition: Nine Elements All Students Should Know, by Mike Ribble. ISTE members save 25% at iste.org/DigCit3E.

5

Digital and Media Literacy

In This Chapter:

4 Ways to Teach Students to Find the Gems in Youtube's Perilous Terrain

5 Things Students Should Do to Stay Safe and Secure Online

Top 10 Sites to Help Students Check Their Facts

Today's News: Real or fake?

Digital and media literacy is a subset of digital citizenship. It's all about accessing, analyzing, evaluating and creating all types of media, from newspaper and magazine articles to tweets, blog posts and YouTube videos.

Having the skills to understand the intentions, biases and motives of the creator is essential in a world where manipulation of facts is easier than ever. Students need to evaluate sources, check facts and recognize red flags to avoid being misled or defrauded.

Media literacy involves more than merely analyzing and evaluating content, though. Students also need these skills to evaluate their own biases and understand their audiences when creating content.

The selections in this chapter offer resources and examples that will help educators train skilled, knowledgeable and informed citizens.

4 Ways to Teach Students to Find the Gems in Youtube's Perilous Terrain

By Adrienne Smith

Today's students constantly seek help from the all-seeing, all-knowing YouTube oracle, much like Dorothy did in the *Wizard of Oz*. Therefore you, the teacher, are no longer seen as the ultimate subject-matter expert. YouTube is.

And that's not necessarily a bad thing.

As practically any adult or child can attest, YouTube can be an excellent tutor, adviser, trip planner, mentor — and, of course, comedian. But it comes with landmines that can be avoided as long as educators and parents know how to find them.

YouTube does not actively monitor videos that are uploaded to the site. They are automatically scanned for copyright infringement, but not inappropriate — or grossly inaccurate — content, unless flagged by a viewer.

Almost Anything Goes on YouTube

Think about that: YouTube, the subject-matter expert in the eyes of students, is a resource that expects the user (a student) to determine the quality of the content. This is a skill that requires students to be Knowledge Constructors as defined by the ISTE Standards for Students. That is, they need a deep understanding of research, curation and critical thinking skills.

Parents have long relied on educators to help their children develop those skills. Along those same lines, colleges/universities and the workforce expect high school graduates to arrive having already developed critical, analytical and evaluative skills.

But students today have 24/7 access to a vast amount of good — and bad — information that requires strong critical thinking skills, and teachers aren't always going to be right behind their shoulders to help them vet content.

Shifting the Teacher's Role

Therefore, teachers must switch from the primary role of subject-matter expert to curriculum facilitator. It is now more important than ever to teach the media literacy skills of analyzing and evaluating.

Learning to think for oneself rather than being told what to think has always been an invaluable skill. As the facilitator, you should encourage your students to take the lead – no more explaining! – and allow students the experience of evaluating. Here are some ways you can do that:

Allow opportunities for controversy. Use YouTube videos to spark thinking and discussion. Teachers have long relied on debate between students as a means of examining arguments and fostering critical thinking. Even a video lacking in depth may be turned into a classroom asset.

English language arts. YouTube is full of reviews and criticism of literature that you can use to spark a discussion. For example, after you finish teaching a text such as Lord of the Flies, show students video reviews and criticism. You can begin a discussion by asking students to brainstorm criteria for judging whether or not the text should be taught in school and at what grade level.

Social Studies. YouTube offers many, many videos depicting differences in perspectives on current events. Search for commentary by ordinary people as well as from media organizations, such as The Blaze, Fox News and CNN. You can trigger interesting discussions relating to viewpoints, voices and groups that are often ignored. Students will be able to recognize that interpretations are influenced by individual experiences and sources selected.

Let students choose the content. Ask students to find YouTube videos they believe will best contribute to understanding the subject being covered in class. This will allow students to develop skills in discernment that will lead them to become lifelong learners and it will help them address the Knowledge Constructor standard within the ISTE Standards for Students.

Math. Give groups of students a complex word problem or an equation than can be solved a variety of ways. Then ask students to find YouTube videos that explain math concepts that can help to solve a word problem or balance an equation. Show the video clips to the class as a whole and allow students to discuss how and why they would or would not solve the problem using the information from each video.

Science. Ask students to find YouTube videos demonstrating experiments related to the scientific concepts being covered in class. Show the experiments to the class and have the students make connections, analyze, synthesize and evaluate the experiments based on the unit of study.

Your role as an instructional facilitator may be even more valuable than your previous role as subject-matter expert. When YouTube is your students' wonderful land of Oz, you need to help each student become a Dorothy who can pull the curtain on the wizard.

This is an updated version of an article that appeared on the ISTE Blog on July 25, 2017.

Adrienne Smith is an educational technology specialist for Pearland Independent School District in Texas and a doctoral candidate at the University of Houston in curriculum and instruction with a focus on learning, design and technology. Follow her on Twitter @ asmithedtech.

5 Things Students Should Do to Stay Safe and Secure Online

By Nicole Zumpano

As adults, we do everything possible to keep our computers, bank accounts and families safe. Our list of to-do's continues to grow as our use of digital technologies increases. While these tasks are rote to most adults, we can't expect that our students will follow our lead.

It's our responsibility as educators to make sure our digital age learners know how to do more than surf the web and consume media. All educators — from classroom teachers to technology coaches and administrators — should lead the discussion on digital literacy.

Here are some ways to make sure our students stay safe and secure online:

Teach Students to Conduct Data Mines (on Themselves)

Students should do this every 3-6 months. While many will Google their names, we need to teach them to dig deeper. Here are some general guidelines to follow:

- Log out of internet browsers before searching (staying logged in can affect the results).

- Search (using quotation marks) full legal names, nicknames and usernames.

- Search Google Images with names/usernames.

- Use multiple browsers, such as Chrome, Bing, Yahoo, Safari and Firefox.

- Look beyond the first page of results. Go at least five pages deep until the name/username no longer appears. Take note of what kind of results appear (presentations/social media/images/etc.).

Here's a link to an exercise I give to graduate students, but it can easily be replicated for high school students: goo.gl/SRe1yM

Check Privacy Settings on Social Media Accounts

Because many sites may be blocked during school hours, allow students to check privacy settings on those that are not. At a minimum, show students how to access privacy settings (perhaps through a screencast or screenshot). On each social media site, students should:

- Check privacy settings to see who can view posts.

- Go through "friends" lists and remove people who should not be there.

- Search posts and remove any that they wouldn't want a parent, teacher, employer or college official to see.

- Look at tagged images that others have posted.

Teach Digital Literacies

Digital literacy is a term that has many moving parts. Students need guidance on varying types of literacy, including media (how to "read" media), social (how to interact in an online environment), and information (the ability to locate, evaluate and properly use information).

Stress the Importance of Digital Maintenance

This is the spelling list or cursive practice of the digital world. It's not glamorous to teach but essential for students to know:

- Teach students how to download Google Drive files to an external drive.

- Remind them to backup Drive files, important emails, smartphone photos/apps/etc. at least once a month.

- Make sure parents have access to account passwords in the event of emergencies. Have them write the accounts/passwords on a piece of paper and place it in an envelope in a safe yet visible place.

- Reiterate the importance of logging out of accounts, not simply closing the browser window.

Start Early

Teaching digital responsibility is not just for middle school or computer lab teachers. It's everyone's duty, and we must start with kindergarteners. Consider developing a digital media scope-and-sequence to address what should be taught at each grade.

This is something that can be developed by teachers, students and parents alike. At a minimum, make a commitment with grade-level colleagues that you'll help teach students how to be safe and secure digital citizens. A good place to begin is by reviewing the ISTE Standards for Students.

This article appeared on the ISTE Blog on Dec. 27, 2017.

Nicole M. Zumpano is a National Board Certified teacher and technology coach in a Chicago Public School as well as an adjunct instructor at three universities. She has master's degrees in instructional technology, and administration and supervision, and is the immediate past president of Illinois Computing Educators, an ISTE affiliate. Read her blog and follow her on Twitter @nmzumpano.

Top 10 Sites to Help Students Check Their Facts

By Jennifer Snelling

In a political climate where sharing fake news has become commonplace, it's more important than ever to rely on trustworthy and dogged fact-checking services to vet information.

Our job as citizens requires more than just being informed. We must also be vigilant about verifying information before posting it on social media. While taking a second look at claims made by politicians and even journalists is a start, we still can't outsource our brains and our judgment, says Tessa Jolls, president of the Center for Media Literacy. "In my view, we have to look as critically at the fact-checking sites as we do the news articles themselves," she says.

A good fact-checking site uses neutral wording, provides unbiased sources to support its claims and reliable links, says Frank Baker, author of Media Literacy in the K-12 Classroom and creator of the Media Literacy Clearinghouse. He adds, "Readers should apply the same critical thinking/questioning to fact-check sites."

Here's a rundown of 10 of the top fact- and bias-checking sites to share with your students:

AllSides. While not a fact-checking site, AllSides curates stories from right-, center- and left-leaning media so that readers can easily compare how bias influences reporting on each topic.

Fact Check. This nonpartisan, nonprofit project of the Annenberg Public Policy Center of the University of Pennsylvania monitors the factual accuracy of what is said by U.S. political players, including politicians, TV ads, debates, interviews and news releases.

Media Matters. This nonprofit and self-described liberal-leaning research center monitors and corrects conservative misinformation in the media.

NewsBusters. A project of the conservative Media Research Center, NewsBusters is focused on "documenting, exposing and neutralizing liberal media bias."

Open Secrets. This nonpartisan, independent and nonprofit website run by the Center for Responsive Politics tracks how much and where candidates get their money.

Politifact. This Pulitzer Prize-winning website rates the accuracy of claims by elected officials. Run by editors and reporters from the independent newspaper Tampa Bay Times, Politicfact features the Truth-O-Meter that rates statements as "True," "Mostly True," "Half True," "False," and "Pants on Fire."

ProPublica. This independent, nonprofit newsroom has won several Pulitzer Prizes, including the 2016 Prize for Explanatory Reporting. ProPublica produces investigative journalism in the public interest.

Snopes. This independent, nonpartisan website run by professional researcher and writer David Mikkelson researches urban legends and other rumors. It is often the first to set the facts straight on wild fake news claims.

The Sunlight Foundation. This nonpartisan, nonprofit organization uses public policy data-based journalism to make politics more transparent and accountable.

Washington Post Fact Checker. Although the Washington Post has a left-center bias, its checks are excellent and sourced. The bias shows up because they fact check conservative claims more than liberal ones.

This is an updated version of an article that appeared on the ISTE Blog on March 8, 2017.

Jennifer Snelling is a freelance writer based in Eugene, Oregon. She writes for ISTE's membership magazine, Empowered Learner, and the ISTE Blog. She is a mom to two digital natives.

Today's News: Real or Fake? (Infographic)

At a time when misinformation and fake news spread like wildfire online, the critical need for media literacy education has never been more pronounced. The evidence is in the data:

- 80% of middle schoolers mistake sponsored content for real news.

- 3 in 4 students can't distinguish between real and fake news on Facebook.

- Fewer than 1 in 3 students are skeptical of biased news sources.

Download the infographic by visiting this link: **http://goo.gl/ArVMRD**

This infographic was published on the ISTE Blog on Nov. 2, 2017.

Check out these other great media literacy resources from ISTE.

"The student's guide to media messages" infographic is a useful reminder to think critically about media messages.
www.iste.org/docs/pdfs/media-literacy-infographic_10-2016.pdf

Media Literacy in the K-12 Classroom, by Frank Baker. ISTE members save 25% at iste.org/MediaLiteracy.

6

Digital Equity

In This Chapter:

Focus on Equity to Ensure That All Students Are 'Computer Science Material'

No Internet at Home? Tap into Your Community to Narrow the Digital Divide

Ensure Equity in Your BYOD Classroom

Maker Movement: Bridging the Gap Between Girls and Stem

Video: Ruha Benjamin: Incubate a Better World in the Minds and Hearts of Students

Webinar: Girls Can Code

Digital equity is a giant umbrella covering different groups of people who depend on educators to advocate on their behalf to ensure no one is left out of the opportunities afforded by the digital age.

Some of those groups include girls and other underrepresented populations in computer science; students in rural communities who lack broadband access; those who live in poor districts that cannot afford the technology tools and teacher training; and students with disabilities who could greatly expand their access to learning if only they had the assistive tools that could help them.

The selections in this section shed light on some of the digital equity issues learners face and offer some ways educators can narrow the digital divide.

Focus on Equity to Ensure That All Students Are 'Computer Science Material'

By Jorge Valenzuela

With the dire need for computer science (CS) skills in today's workforce, one would think that every school in the nation would have a robust CS program. But sadly, almost half of U.S. students do not have access to meaningful CS courses in their schools, and many will graduate from the K-12 system unprepared for life after school.

Those most at risk of being left out will be students who don't see themselves as "computer science material" – girls, African Americans and Latinos. That's why there's a critical need for schools to provide equitable access to all learners, and the call to action echoes all the way from the U.S. Department of Education to the bipartisan CTE Excellence and Equity Act, which aims to redesign American high schools.

But what does equity in computer science (CS) education look like? And how can you ensure all of your students are being served? Here are three ways you can work toward CS equity in your school or district.

1. Strategically Plan How You Will Provide CS Access to All

CS equity does not mean that computer science takes place in one class or course. Equity in CS requires an equity mindset and whole-school approach. Schools that identify teacher leaders and relevant CS pathways will have the most impact. That'll ensure that both teaching and learning occur equitably, in succession and effectively.

Not sure how to get started? There are a number of organizations to turn to for help.

Code.org is a nonprofit dedicated to expanding access to computer science and increasing participation by women and underrepresented minorities. It offers an abundance of free CS curriculum and professional development resources.

K-12 Computer Science Framework is a reputable source for equity in CS. It offers strategies for weaving equity into teaching, recruiting and development of classroom culture practices.

CSforAll Consortium provides a central resource for people interested in CS education to find providers, schools, funders and researchers focused on the goal of providing quality CS education to every child in the U.S.

There are also many other resources and DIY guides for educators to get started.

2. Know Your Students, Their Needs and Their Challenges

Creating a classroom culture based on deep mastery of the core practices in CS (including computational thinking) requires educators to take equitable and practical steps toward learning objectives and intended outcomes for all students.

As a 21st century society, we've widely accepted the notion that rights and freedoms of expression, beliefs and pursuits are for all. Unfortunately, for some, this is just lip service. Sadly, this negatively impacts many of our students and can cause them to lack awareness of CS offerings at their schools, prevent them from discovering their interests and passions, and preclude them from developing mastery in the core CS practices.

It is common for students who don't see CS as an option — or are perceived by the adults as not CS material — to slip through the cracks. Unfortunately, this type of exclusion often happens to students who belong to a particular gender or race. A report exploring diversity gaps in CS by the underrepresentation of girls, African American and Hispanics suggests that many of these students are less likely to be encouraged toward CS, have limited access to CS classes and, as a result, lack interest in CS. The report suggests that only when schools and educators understand the real challenges and obstacles affecting young people in CS and intentionally practice equity in recruitment practices will they significantly improve student satisfaction and retention.

Equity in recruitment practices can be remedied by either mandating a CS course, a sequence of CS courses or simply by incorporating CS into the existing curriculum (where it fits logically). My state of Virginia was the first to make CS education mandatory, and many states and departments of education are working toward making similar strides.

3. Become a Facilitator of Equity

Facilitation is a skill that teachers should add to their equity toolkit for effectively engaging students in learning both CS and collaboration with peers. When educators let go of the need to govern every aspect of how a lesson is learned and delivered, students who are typically left out have a chance to shine. Some learners may lack confidence, are being bullied, struggle with identity, lack a sense of belonging, are experiencing hardships, have learning disabilities, lack social skills, have gaps in knowledge or only just need to develop their voice.

The key here is to remove the isolation that often impedes the social and academic success of our students. By structuring CS learning experiences within projects and requiring students to work together, educators can more effectively make the transition from owners of knowledge to facilitators of knowledge. The project-based learning (PBL) instructional approach is excellent for making this happen and schools are increasingly using it as an agent for equity and for developing students' empathy and global citizenship.

It's also important to note that facilitation must be balanced with sufficient planning, direct instruction and classroom management. Any intended CS learning must align to standards and requires teachers to be aware of the content (albeit, not necessarily be experts), be comfortable with the use of the integrated technology tools and know the potential challenges students may face while working collaboratively. For this purpose, the K-12 CS Learning Framework and the ISTE Standards for Students are excellent resources to help teachers plan projects and lessons for empowering students to take ownership of their learning.

It's not About Us; It's About Them

Lastly, when thinking about equity, remember the words of the late Rita F. Pierson Ed.D., "Every child deserves a champion; an adult who will never give up on them, who understands the power of connection and insists that they become the best they can possibly be."

Many of our kids will come to us with a variety of circumstances that aren't always conducive for them to put their best foot forward. The fact of the matter is they can thrive, they just have to learn how. That's where we come in. Our teaching (whether it's CS or not) should always be equitable and never be about us. It needs to begin with us in becoming what we want to see in the students.

This is an updated version of an article that was published on the ISTE Blog on Dec. 7, 2017.

Jorge Valenzuela is a graduate teaching assistant and doctoral student at Old Dominion University, a national faculty of the Buck Institute for Education and a national teacher effectiveness coach with the International Technology and Engineering Educators Association (ITEEA). Connect with Valenzuela on Twitter @JorgeDoesPBL.

No Internet at Home? Tap into Your Community to Narrow the Digital Divide

By Julie Randles

Just four years ago, the Rowan-Salisbury School System in Salisbury, North Carolina, put devices in the hands of 19,500 K-12 students. Learners in grades 3-12 brought the devices home every day. Almost immediately, an issue arose.

Despite every student having a device, a digital divide still existed.

Sixty-five percent of Rowan-Salisbury students receive free and reduced-price lunch, thanks in part to the textile industry — which once employed much of the community — moving overseas. When these students went home, poverty existed and access to the internet often didn't.

In an effort to address the digital divide, the school system reached out to the community for solutions, said Andrew Smith, the district's chief strategy officer. The core question: How do we make internet access available outside of school so students can use their devices to study, do research and complete homework?

"We said 'We can't tackle this alone, we need community partners,'" Smith said. The district knew that its 1:1 computing initiative would go a long way toward improving literacy — but not until all students had connectivity even after they stepped off the school bus.

The partnerships and solutions took many forms, until they eventually found 75 Wi-Fi hotspots in both urban and rural areas of the community. Now the goal is to establish 25 more for a total of 100.

Here's how Rowan-Salisbury Schools attacked the problem:

The literacy summits. Over the past three years, business, community and church leaders were invited to a summit where the district laid out its literacy plan, explained its 1:1 initiative and asked for help. Nearly 500 people have attended the meetings. District representatives explained how the digital divide impacts student achievement and asked those in attendance to help them address the access issues many students face at home.

The challenge. Superintendent Lynn Moody challenged those who operated businesses in the community to provide students with free internet access so they could stop by and do their homework. In return, the district would spotlight the businesses on its website and provide window clings identifying the locations as Wi-Fi hotspots for area students.

The churches. With a couple solutions in place for urban students, the district turned to rural areas where students faced geographical internet poverty. The district approached faith-based groups and asked them to consider opening church doors to students after school.

Simultaneously, the district contacted an internet provider and a cable provider to collaborate on providing connectivity for the rural church buildings. Churches were asked to provide access to students two or three hours a week. It didn't take long for some to agree to offer an hour or so every day. In some cases, having the students on site has provided churches with opportunities for new ministries and provide meals.

The libraries. The district adjusted library hours at schools, keeping them open later in the day so kids could do homework after school.

The teachers. Teachers were trained to deal with classrooms where only half the students had internet access at home. Educators were asked to evaluate the efficacy of the homework they assigned to ensure it was valuable. They also learned about apps students could use at home that don't require connectivity, and they were encouraged to have students download materials at school so they could work offline at home.

The district. District officials asked vendors to offer digital resources that function offline. Whether a learning management system, a literacy program or a general digital content resource, vendors were told, "If you don't have an offline function, we don't want to talk to you."

The buses. A wildly successful summer food program led to another innovative solution. This summer, the district's nutrition department served 85,000 meals to students out of remodeled school buses parked throughout the community, which got Smith thinking. What if we fitted buses with a wireless hotspot and served dinner from the buses during the school year? That plan is in the works and the district now has four "Yum Yum" buses.

The mobile hotspots. Thanks to a generous donation and partnership with Community in Schools, the district was able to purchase 300 wireless routers that act as mobile Wi-Fi hotspots, along with monthly data plans. The majority of the 300 devices are given to the most impoverished students throughout the district for nightly use. A smaller subset of devices were given to each media center to be loaned to any student who may need them for sporadic usage.

"Some of the most simple solutions that you can implement tomorrow don't take any money at all," Smith said. "There's no one solution that solves all of the problems. It becomes a mix of all solutions."

This is an updated version of an article published on the ISTE Blog on July 27, 2015.

Julie Phillips Randles is a freelance writer and editor with 30 years of experience writing about education policy, leadership, curriculum and edtech.

Ensure Equity in Your BYOD Classroom

By Liz Kolb

The bring-your-own-device (BYOD) movement in K-12 schools has skyrocketed over the past five years. In fact, about 83 percent of U.S. school districts have policies, or plan to have policies, allowing student devices to be used in the classroom for learning. But BYOD is often dependent on students using whatever technology they have at home, most often a cellphone.

And although most teenagers own a cellphone, the fact is, not all phones are created equal; functionality and phone plans vary widely. While 73 percent of teens have access to a smartphone, 15 percent have only a basic phone and 12 percent have no phone at all. That means that activities requiring mobile apps or storage of large amounts of data are not accessible for all students.

That's why it's important for teachers to select activities that both they and all of their students can do using any phone or phone plan. So before creating activities, make sure to survey students about their phones and phone plans.

In general, all phones can text and make phone calls. Below are three ways to connect learning with any phone.

1. Text Alerts

Text alerts are messages that go out to an entire group, such as students, parents or both. Alerts can be one-way (teacher to student), two-way private (teacher to student to teacher) or two-way open (teacher to student to students/teacher). Here are some pedagogical strategies for using text alerts to enhance learning:

> **Managerial.** Send quick announcements, such as homework reminders or upcoming class activities. It's usually one way from the teacher to the student or teacher to parent.

Project-based. Use the alert as a way for students to produce or participate in a classroom project. For example, an English teacher might ask her students to text an original poem for an assignment along with a visual image of what inspired the poem. Or a social studies teacher might create a virtual debate where students can text back and forth in the voice of a historical character.

Small group. Put students into groups based on their reading and mathematics levels or academic interests and then send tailored messages to those groups. In addition, you can open up the groups (two-way texting) so that they can text back and forth with other group members to collaborate, brainstorm or even create virtual book clubs.

Polling. Send a multiple-choice or free-response poll to students during class. The students can text an immediate response. These are helpful as quick exit tickets, share-outs or basic feedback.

Tutor. Send one-way alerts to help with FAQs during a class activity. You can also assign an older student to send out tutoring help to younger students. Do this by setting up a tutoring line (two-way private), where students can text when they need help and an older student or adult volunteer can text back helpful hints or tips.

Text pals. Pair students with students in a similar grade/classroom from another school. By using the two-way private text alerts, students can learn from each other as pen pals. You can be on the two-way alert to monitor the conversation.

Field trips. Send out a two-way alert during field trips with an activity or poll asking the students to text back their work, such as sending in an interesting fact or image.

Assessments. Use the two-way private alerts to send quick surveys, polls or quizzes to better understand how well each student comprehends a topic. The responses return to you in a private texting file online. Now you have an archive of the quick assessments that you can use to personalize learning.

Personalizing. Send out private alerts to specific groups or students to help scaffold their learning during a class assignment. For example, if a student finishes a class activity quickly, ask her to respond with a summary of how she was able to solve the mathematics problem and the reasoning she used.

Here is a handful of tools to help you create text alerts:

Remind. Teachers can use this tool to schedule text messages in advance. This works great for weekly homework or prescheduling in-class alerts. You can even schedule tweets and send with attachments. It's a great tool for one-way alerts.

Joopz. This is an easy way to do multiple group messaging. You can toggle between different classes or groups set up for various alerts. You can also schedule and archive messages.

ClassPager. This tool presents the alert feedback from students graphically. For example, if you text students asking them to vote on an issue, the results will show up in a pie chart.

2. Moblogging

Some websites allow students to create a new blog post via texting — aka moblogging. Moblogging is an inclusive option for students to publish digital journals, and it creates opportunities for authentic, real-time collaboration. Below are pedagogical examples of how you can use moblogging to enhance learning:

Field trips. Students can live-blog from their phones about their off-campus experiences rather than waiting until they get back to the classroom. Parents and community members can read the blog as students post live updates!

Classroom reflections. When students are working in groups during class, it's sometimes difficult to know what learning is occurring in each group. Ask students in each group to reflect (via moblog) on their activities as they work so you can offer quick feedback and allow students to review their collaboration.

Ebooks. There are online resources where students can write and publish a piece of literary work using their phones.

Here are a few tools for moblogging:

Blogger, WordPress and Tumblr. These blogging platforms allow students to text directly to the blog from an email address.

Twitter. Students and teachers can text to post on Twitter and receive messages and updates on any Twitter feed.

3. Phone Calling

One feature of every phone is calling. There are numerous possibilities to connect voice to classroom learning, including:

Podcasting. Students can call in a live podcast on a topic of research. Podcasting directly to the internet from a phone is easier than traditional podcasting because you don't need to upload a file to a host. You can also do it from anywhere.

Interviews and oral histories. Students conduct interviews to record the experiences of their peers and other community members. Capturing oral histories directly from a phone is appealing because students can conduct their interviews in historical locations.

Discipline discourse. Students call to record their explanations of subject-area concepts or how they arrived at answers in a discipline of study (such as solving a mathematics answer).

Salon/debate. In contrast to an in-class debate where some students may be nervous to speak in front of their peers, a phone-conferencing tool allows for full participation that archives each person's speaking role in the debate.

Here are some online tools for phone recording:

Google Voice. With this tool, teachers can get a local phone number that they can give to students and parents. Teachers can record voicemail messages for all their students or different groups of students to hear when they call in. Students can leave voicemail messages that become MP3 downloadable files.

iPadio. This tool allows you to broadcast a recording directly from your phone. The podcasts can be public or private. iPadio has speech-to-text transcription.

FreeConferencePro. This allows large-group phone conferencing. With one phone call, you can set up a phone conference with up to 200 callers and archive it.

Talkshoe. Students can live-broadcast from their phones. The broadcast can include "guest callers" who call in to the broadcast, just like an authentic radio show.

Hipcast. With this tool, anyone can call and record a podcast that posts directly to the internet. Recordings are archived and can be turned into a playlist as well as downloadable MP3 files.

This is an updated version of an article published on the ISTE Blog on June 16, 2015.

Liz Kolb is a clinical associate at The University of Michigan in Ann Arbor, Michigan. She is the author of the ISTE book Learning First, Technology Second. She is also the inventor and coordinator of the 4T Virtual Conference, a free annual conference for practitioners. Kolb is a former social studies and computer technology teacher who spent four years as a technology coordinator and integration specialist in Ohio.

Maker Movement: Bridging the Gap Between Girls and STEM

By Lisa Abel-Palmieri

Girls want to change the world.

Eighty-eight percent say they want to make a difference with their lives, and 90 percent express a desire to help people, according to the Girl Scouts' "Generation STEM" research. Girls have traditionally achieved this goal through people-oriented careers rather than through applying technology and scientific expertise to change the way things are done.

However, if more girls learn that STEM careers open up new avenues to help and serve, more girls will choose STEM.

Maker education allows girls to experience in a fun, tangible way how they can apply STEM skills to solve real problems — all while developing dexterity, learning about ideation and practicing teamwork. By giving girls the opportunity to make and tinker, we also help them develop their creative confidence so they persevere in pursuing STEM majors and careers.

The "Generation STEM" report found that 92 percent of girls who engage with STEM subjects believe they are smart enough to pursue a career in STEM — versus 68 percent of girls who don't display an interest in science, technology, engineering or math.

To nudge girls toward making and tinkering, "include things that are attractive to girls. Robots are great, but think about other things — or let your robot be a helper bot," says Laura Blankenship, co-founder of the #MakerEd chat on Twitter.

Andrew Carle, another founder of #MakerEd chat, advises educators to "start early, when a child's enthusiasm and aptitude can still drown out ingrained gender expectations."

Through using design thinking and maker education, girls at The Ellis School are empowered to identify for themselves what problems and challenges in their community and life they want to address, rather than having these challenges defined for them. Maker education at Ellis enriches the curricular program in a really hands-on way that builds critical thinking skills and fosters creativity.

Here are a few examples of how The Ellis School integrates maker education throughout all grade levels:

Innovation stations. More than two years ago, we launched innovation stations in all classrooms in the lower school and in common areas in the middle and upper schools with the goal of providing girls a place to explore and tinker in a nonthreatening way. From building wind turbines to using Makey-Makey to write music and program Hummingbird robots, girls have fun while making.

One middle school innovation station features an activity in which the girls build an origami character that has LEDs and motors (using the Invent-abling kit). They then write a short creative piece about the character, take a picture and post it to an origami gallery. This activity incorporates literature, arts and STEM.

Tinkering is a powerful form of learning by doing, an ethos shared by the rapidly expanding maker movement community as well as many educators. Real science and engineering are done through tinkering.

Artificial limb lab. In our upper school engineering design class, the girls worked on an artificial limb lab. Faculty who co-teach the class mentored small teams of three to four students as they identified problems people with disabilities face, developed empathy for people facing these disabilities through personal stories and research, and designed multiple iterations of their solutions with Autodesk Inventor. They used the MakerBot Replicator 3D printer, along with manual tools, to make prototypes. The teams then printed final parts on the 3D printer and presented them to the class and an internal panel.

Projects included the "RecFin," an assistive swimming device for people with a limb loss below the knee; the "Triple Threat," an assistive hair-tying device; the "BAZAD," a button and zipping assistive device; and the "Hold Tight," a device to help grip small objects.

Metropolitan Community Project. Our second grade students created a model of a metropolitan community. Serving as city planners, they made decisions about the placement of services, taking into consideration issues such as aesthetics, usage, space restraints, noise and pollution. The girls also gave special attention to green building and planning.

They worked in cooperative learning groups to design and construct streets, bridges, trams, tunnels, an incline, parking facilities, signage, parks and recreational spaces. As neighborhoods and services sprang up, the girls positioned single-family homes as well as townhouses, apartment houses and duplexes they made with a partner.

CoLaboratory and Active Classroom for Girls. Students helped us design and launch an Active Classroom for Girls and a CoLaboratory. The project combines innovative teaching methods — such as the flipped classroom, design thinking and maker education — with physics and engineering courses.

Lectures are predominately online and students spend class time collaborating in groups to define and solve problems through hands-on experiments and making. We intentionally built in time for girls to develop empathy for each other as well as others in our community and across the globe, all while applying risk-taking and perseverance to solve challenges.

Maker education strengthens girls' capacity for problem solving, collaboration and creative confidence. Making puts girls in charge of their learning — and in many cases this requires a cultural shift around how schools approach learning.

This is an updated version of an article published on the ISTE Blog on March 22, 2014

Lisa Abel-Palmieri, Ph.D., is the head of school and chief learning officer at Holy Family Academy. Connect with her on Twitter @Learn21Tech.

Video: Ruha Benjamin: Incubate a Better World in the Minds and Hearts of Students

Ruha Benjamin sees schools as laboratories of democratic participation, where society incubates a better world in the hearts and minds of its students.

The Princeton professor who specializes in the interdisciplinary study of science, medicine, biotechnology, race, ethnicity and gender, health and bio politics, believes that teachers, if unified and empowered, can change the direction of history.

In her hour-long speech delivered at ISTE 2016, Benjamin said the first step to creating a society where people care and sacrifice for one another is to examine whose version of the good life is setting the standards — and whose voices are being ignored. Real power, she contends, lies with who gets to dream today, including the lower income and minority students in our classrooms.

Include everyone. One bright bulb does not enlightenment make, Benjamin assured. Placeholders aren't inclusion. Make sure the weaker contributors still have a chance to participate and master their potential, too.

Watch the entire speech here: **www.youtube.com/watch?v=9xmrJJESCt8&feature= youtu.be**

Webinar: Girls Can Code

In this 30-minute webinar, Tara Linney of the ISTE Global Collaboration Network and an educational technology coach at Singapore American School, addresses issues related to girls and coding, including gender equality in the computer science fields, female role models in STEM subjects and gender equity in school coding programs.

She explains the United Nations' sustainable development goals — 17 goals for making the world a better, more equitable place — particularly those related to gender equity. A big part of those goals relate to the use of and access to technology.

Linney offers educators strategies for how they can do their part to end gender inequities in STEM fields by exposing girls to female scientists and engaging them STEM projects.

Download Adobe Connect and then watch the full webinar with this link: **https://iste.adobeconnect.com/_a729309453/p1frb47ovzgw/?proto=true**

Resources

Check out these other digital equity resources from ISTE.

Learning Supercharged, by Lynne Schrum and Sandi Sumerfield. ISTE members save 25% at iste.org/LearningSupercharged.

See what ISTE members are saying and join the conversation in the Digital Equity community at community.iste.org/home.

7

Digital Learning Lessons and Resources

In This Chapter:

Can Minecraft Teach Team Building?

25 Resources for Bringing AR And VR to the Classroom

Coding in the Elementary School Classroom

Students Create Tech Tutorials to Teach Each Other

5 Ways to Use Memes With Students

TPACK as a Tool for Professional Learning

Once you get a sense of when and why to use technology in the classroom, you need to focus on how to use it. There are endless tools, methods and strategies you can choose from. As long as your lessons are aligned to the ISTE Standards, there are a variety of ways you can tailor your lessons to meet the diverse needs and passions of all your students.

The articles in this chapter offer a few examples of how you can use technology in a way that empowers learners and sets them up for success in their future careers and lives.

Can Minecraft Teach Team Building?

By Douglas Kiang

It was October. My Introduction to Computer Science class had been meeting for two months and we were deep into a discussion about game design. One of my students gestured casually at the student across the room. "That's right! I agree with what … what's-his-name said over there."

I was shocked. After the first week of classes, I knew all my students' names. But our high school is so big that many students had few opportunities to interact. In my classroom, I ask kids to help each other find solutions to the problems they come across. That's difficult when they don't know each other very well.

I wanted to come up with a way for students to build community, so I decided to set up a classroom server and assign students to play Minecraft together. I wanted to see if playing the game would provide some scaffolding for team building.

Minecraft is an online 3D fantasy world where students build structures using digital blocks of glass, sand, brick and other materials. I used this popular game as a virtual ropes course that would allow kids to work together to solve challenges. If two kids go into the mountains and bring me back an iron ax, I know they have spent several hours watching each other's back, going into dangerous areas and developing the technology to smelt raw iron ore into bars to make that ax. It is a tangible artifact representing hours of teamwork.

What I really wanted to find out though was if this digital collaborative experience would translate to the face-to-face classroom. If kids learn to work together in a virtual environment, would they watch each other's backs in the real world? Would it make them more willing to admit to each other that they didn't understand something? By using Minecraft as a virtual world co-existing in tandem with my classroom environment, I hoped to my students would develop strong working relationships while helping each other build houses, tackle community projects and make their world sustainable.

The Minecraft experience is fun and engaging, but it is also a catalyst for powerful learning. As a teacher, many of my biggest "teachable moments" — when we learn about civility and community and doing the right thing — actually occur when the laptops are closed and we are able to talk as a group about what's happening. These lessons are inspired by Minecraft, but the good teaching occurs face to face.

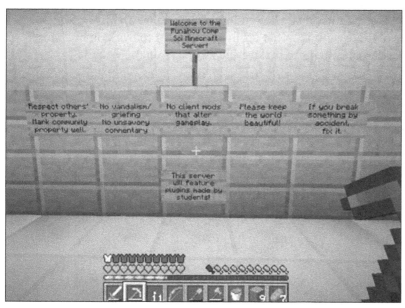

Figure 7.1. Student-created community in Minecraft.

Making the Rules

I challenged students to build and maintain an entire community and village that would parallel their experience in the face-to-face classroom. The mission for our Minecraft world was to "create a self-sustaining community that reinforces trust between individuals and rewards prosocial behavior." Students were expected to ask themselves at every point, "Does what I'm about to do create or destroy trust? Will it help my community?"

Some students argued that if we were to live together, we would need a strong set of rules, consequences for breaking them and some way to enforce those penalties. For example, breaking something another student built would result in being banned. Other students disagreed, saying that we could set up the server so that students physically couldn't alter anything they did not own.

This led to a great debate about whether we should let technology control our actions or whether we should be allowed to make mistakes and live with the consequences of those actions. What if I invite you over to work on my house? Can we trust external systems to make ethical choices on our behalf?

Figure 7.2. Rules for Minecraft community.

Ultimately we decided to come up with some basic rules:

- Don't damage other people's things.

- If you break something by accident, fix it.

- Keep the world beautiful.

Getting Along

Once our world was up and running, students built all sorts of constructions that helped the community. Farms sprouted up across the landscape to provide food in case of emergency (if you don't eat in Minecraft, you will die). Players created a community chest for others to take from or add to, as necessary. Surprisingly, they soon needed to add a second chest because people were leaving more than they took.

Figure 7.3. Work of art or eyesore? Students debate civic issues in Minecraft.

One student traveled around the landscape building enormous statues and billboards with cartoon characters. His creativity was impressive, but some students complained:

"I selected this site to build my house because it had a beautiful view of the ocean," one student said. "Now I have to stare at the back of Winnie the Pooh's head. Make him stop!"

"OK," I replied. "But what rule is he breaking? We have rules against destroying things, but not against building things." This puzzled my students for a while, until one spoke up.

"Keep the world beautiful! That's a rule!"

"OK, I'll just have him take down the ugly sculptures like the giant snake."

Other students objected. "Wait! That's the only beautiful thing he did! Take down the giant statue instead!"

"No, that one's not so bad, but the billboard has got to go!"

We decided that judging the beauty of public art was difficult. We designated a public park away from residential areas where all could admire his work.

This episode turned out to be a powerful learning experience. "I just realized something," said one student who approached me later. "In the beginning, we had a hard time coming up with rules because no one knew what was going to happen. Now I think that laws only exist because someone at some point in the past did something before it was a law."

Making Real-World Parallels

Another debate occurred over the use of TNT, a Minecraft block that can destroy large areas of the world. Some students argued that TNT should be banned from the classroom world because of the tremendous damage it could do if it were misused, and because "no one needs explosives that powerful."

Other students created a petition to keep TNT in the game. After all, they argued, it is a timesaver when clearing large areas of land, and "I have the right to use it responsibly."

One student was so agitated that he sent an impassioned email pleading with me not to take away his large stash of TNT. If it's misused, he said, "Ban the user, not the material!!!"

Every student had an opinion. When I pointed out the numerous parallels to our national debate over gun control, internet filtering and regulation of hazardous substances, the conversation spilled over into the real world. "I didn't really know that much about those issues," one student admitted. "But I feel like I'll definitely pay more attention to them now."

Great teachable moments, all inspired by Minecraft, but delivered face to face.

I was fascinated by other ways the virtual world spilled over into the real world as well. For example, instead of giving points for extra credit, which I have never been entirely comfortable with, I started awarding diamonds to students who went "above and beyond." Although diamonds are a rare resource in the Minecraft world, they cost me nothing to produce and have no impact on my grade book. Yet they were just as powerful an incentive. I also found that students would sometimes give enchanted tools and potions as a "thank you" to other students who had helped them in class during the day.

Building Trust in the Minecraft Community

At first, I thought I could use Minecraft to teach lessons about physics or electricity, but I was stymied by some of the quirky physics involved. Minecraft follows its own set of rules. In the end, I realized that teaching content in Minecraft was not nearly as important as building the relationships and collaboration skills that would sustain my students when we started studying heavily for the AP exam in the second semester.

Minecraft offers powerful lessons in collaboration and relationship building. Students learn how the Minecraft world works, then tackle big, difficult problems within that game world. At every step, Minecraft offers the promise of building or creating something that has never been done before, using skills and partnerships that players have developed over time.

Because the server was up 24/7, my students played Minecraft outside school hours. I gave them assignments to complete, but during our class meetings, we studied course content, enhanced by my students' willingness to help each other. The experiences led to successful interactions in their face-to-face learning because the students knew and trusted each other on a level that I had not previously seen.

The power of Minecraft as a catalyst for learning is in its ability to involve students in creating a shared world together, in all of its intricacies and challenges and difficult conversations.

Good teachers are at the heart of this process, not just for providing a powerful learning environment to students, but also for helping them create meaning from the challenges they face and the choices they make. This teaching can take place when the laptops are closed, face to face. As students become better citizens in the virtual world, so will they develop powerful skills for negotiation and compromise that serve them well in the real world.

This is an updated version of an article that published on the ISTE Blog on Sept. 16, 2014.

Douglas Kiang is an Apple Distinguished Educator with over 20 years of teaching experience at the elementary, middle and high school levels. He teaches computer science at Punahou School in Honolulu, Hawaii, and holds a master's degree in technology, innovation and education from Harvard.

25 Resources for Bringing AR and VR to the Classroom

By Jennifer Snelling

Affordable tools like Google Cardboard are Aurasma are making virtual and augmented reality (VR and AR) the hottest thing in edtech. If you haven't yet dabbled in AR or VR and don't get the appeal, imagine studying underwater ecosystems and taking the whole class scuba diving with just a smartphone and a $6 headset.

The benefits include increased engagement and shared experience among students. Although the immersive experience is enhanced with a headset, the 360-degree experience is still worth exploring. Teachers can take advantage of many of the VR apps using the individual laptops, iPads or electronic whiteboards already in the classroom. While VR is changing quickly, the resources below are a good starting point.

360cities (360cities.net): Where do your students want to go? Just type in Rome, Tokyo, London and tour anyplace in the world with a 360-degree view. Free.

4D Anatomy (4danatomy.com): Subscription-based app allows students to explore human anatomy.

Alchemy VR (alchemyvr.com) has partnered with Expeditions to produce experiences narrated by naturalist David Attenborough. Otherwise, schools can purchase their own kits for $4,000 for 10 kits.

AugThat (augthat.com): Features a large content-based augmented virtual reality library.

Aurasma (aurasma.com): Free app lets teachers create their own AR auras for their classrooms.

Boulevard (blvrd.com): This app lets you explore art galleries all over the world.

Curioscope (curioscope.com): This innovative platform has one person wear a T-shirt while the other uses a smartphone to launch the app and learn about the human body in a whole new way.

Discovery VR (discoveryvr.com): Discovery has added a VR app that allows you to experience your favorite Discovery programs, such as Deadliest Catch or Mythbusters in VR.

EON Reality (eonreality.com/solutions/education): Students and teachers can create a blended-learning environment that allows creators to combine 3D with PowerPoint, notes, sound effects and more.

Immersive VR Education (immersivevreducation.com): Free education platform allows teachers to create their own lesson plans and immersive experiences.

ISTE Librarian's Network Webinar: Elissa Malespina, author of *Augmented Reality in Education: Bringing Interactivity to Libraries and Classrooms* has created a webinar about using AR and VR in the classroom. Watch at **youtube.com/watch?v=Jxf6VxvWXAo&feature=youtu.be.**

Google Cardboard (vr.google.com/cardboard): Inexpensive headset that sells for under $10 and works with smartphone VR apps.

Google Expeditions AR Pioneer Program (edu.google.com/expeditions/#about): With Google Expeditions kits you'll have everything you need to take students on a virtual field trip anywhere, from an underwater coral reef to Machu Picchu. But the kits aren't cheap. They cost $4,000 for a set of 10.

Mattel View-Master Virtual Reality Viewer: At $17, this viewer costs a little more than the Cardboard, but it's made of plastic and might last a little longer. Available on Amazon.com.

Minecraft Education Edition (education.minecraft.net): The popular game has an education version that allows students to create their own virtual world, such as Jamestown or Fort Clatsop.

Nearpod (nearpod.com): This is a free-for-teachers VR-based curriculum.

Pokemon Go (pokemongo.com): Use this mobile app to teach mapping and community-oriented learning.

Quiver (quivervision.com): Bring coloring to life with augmented reality content in biology, geometry and the solar system. App is less than $10.

Schell Games (schellgames.com): Engaging game experiences designed to positively impact a person's habits, attitudes or knowledge.

Thinglink (thinglink.com): Subscription-based program allows teachers to create interactive images and videos.

Timelooper (timelooper.com): Free app allows students to go back in time in London, from medieval times to World War II.

Unimersiv (unimersiv.com): This individualized and immersive learning platform releases content on a monthly basis.

Wild Eyes (putonyourwildeyes.com): If your students are excited about VR, maybe they will want to support this campaign to fund a virtual tour of the nation's National Parks.

YouTube 360 (youtube.com/360): Explore the streets of Paris or the trails of the Grand Canyon with free videos shot with a 360-degree camera.

zSpace (zspace.com): Offers different STEM programs, including Euclid's shapes or human anatomy at various prices.

This is an updated version of an article published on the ISTE Blog on July 27, 2015.

Jennifer Snelling is a freelance writer based in Eugene, Oregon, and mom to two digital natives.

Coding in the Elementary School Classroom

By Janice Mak

My goal as an educator is to lead my students to new ways of thinking, understanding and communicating in a digital world. I know that if I teach my students basic coding, they will be on their way to learning those skills and have a good time doing it. But I didn't expect this breathless comment to spill out of the mouth of one of my third graders after I taught her to use Scratch.

"I just started coding, and it is like a new world!" she said. "It is amazing because you get to almost go into someone else's brain and teach them based on how they think."

When I heard those words, I realized my students were learning much more than just HTML. Since starting my journey with the Coding is Common to the Core initiative in the Paradise Valley Unified School District in Phoenix, Arizona, I've looked for innovative ways to implement the ISTE Standards for Students and the Common Core State Standards (CCSS) while teaching my students to code.

I started the year with Scratch, giving my students design-based challenges to familiarize them with the basic blocks. For example, after a lesson on idioms, I had the students create an animation in Scratch to illustrate an idiom. They unleashed their imagination while demonstrating understanding and mastery of a concept.

Next, they would reflect on and analyze the thinking they used while programming. Here's how one of my fourth graders described his experience using Scratch:

> I am working on an idiom project — a taste of your own medicine. It was pretty challenging because most of the sprites they had were not what I needed so I had to create my own and my own background and fix things up and reprogram it to make it better. I had to make my mad scientist disappear. When I was trying to do that, I tried to make my own block and typed in "disappear," but when I clicked on that for him, he just stayed there. Then I had to make him move 240 steps so you didn't see him anymore, but you could still see his hand. I'm trying to make him "disappear," but it's hard because I tried to get the background to go over him, but that didn't work either (so) … I'm looking around Scratch to see how I can program it to set itself up all over again.

Real-World Debugging Experience

Next, I gave my students a series of debugging challenges, beginning with some created by MIT's Scratch Ed team. This gave them exposure to the process of solving glitches, and it simulated the experiences of computer scientists working in the real world. Being put in a situation where they were "stuck" spontaneously led my students to a paired-programming approach that involved communication and collaboration with their peers. Instead of struggling independently on complex tasks, they asked one another for ideas and leads to solve the challenges.

For a performance-based assessment, I started a studio in Scratch called Mak's Debuggers (although one student recently suggested I change it to Mak's Exterminators), where my students created and submitted their own debug-it programs for their classmates.

Scratch also allows students to tinker with existing projects. Using the remix feature, they can redesign another student's project, adding their own touches and personality while learning from others in an informal but authentic way.

As the students worked on their Scratch projects, I also taught some basic computer science concepts, such as binary numbers, so that students would better understand how computers work and refine their computational thinking.

Beginning with a mini-lesson on binary numbers, I asked them to connect what they learned to the eight standards for mathematical practice in the CCSS. Here's how one of the third graders responded:

In binary numbers, I use math practice number 6 (attend to precision) when doing code. Binary numbers are the digits 0 and 1. Code for binary numbers is doubling one number starting with one and writing them in 0 or 1. You see, trying binary numbers with cards makes it easier. We did it in class once. First, our teacher made us cards that say 1, 2, 4, 8, and 16. Cards that are showing are 1. Cards that are not are 0. Then our teacher, Mrs. Mak, said a number and we had to put the cards face-down if they did not equal the number Mrs. Mak said. For example, if all the cards were showing and we had to make the number 12, then we would flip over 16, 2, and 1 so that only numbers that are showing are 8 and 4 because if you add them together, you get 12. So in binary, it would be 01100. You have to attend to precision when doing binary numbers.

For more ideas on teaching about computer science "unplugged," I have found CSunplugged and Code.org to be outstanding resources.

Robotics Teach Problem-Solving

NXT Mindstorms, LEGO's programmable robot kit, is another powerful tool that fosters critical thinking, problem-solving and collaboration. I began by setting up a series of challenges for my students, such as having the robot travel accurately in a straight line from a starting point to the finish line. We then moved on to more complex robot obstacle courses involving mazes and figure eights.

It was amazing to see my students ask one another questions, engage in mathematical reasoning, and even argue over the best way to complete the challenge. They pulled out rulers, measuring tapes and calculators. Then they debated the merits of programming the robot using number of rotations, time in number of seconds or number of degrees.

The most valuable discussions occurred when students did not experience immediate success. Rather than step in with the answer, I asked more questions to ignite their thinking. For example, when they saw that the robot traveled only about half the length of the course, they began to investigate by tracing back through their steps to see where their programming had gone awry.

They discovered the importance of being consistent with the systems of measurement. Instead of measuring the circumference of the robot's tires in inches, as they had done with the length of the course, they measured it in centimeters. These learning experiences make indelible impressions on my students as they persevered in solving problems collaboratively.

Computational thinking is not just for an elite group of students who enroll as computer science majors in universities. I have seen every one of my students, regardless of gender or background, benefit from the thinking and collaboration that is inherent in what we do in the classroom. It flows seamlessly into the CCSS and ISTE Standards. The ultimate goal, after all, is to cultivate critical thinkers who can deconstruct problems into their component parts to solve them effectively, communicate their findings, and justify their reasoning with evidence.

In the words of one of my fourth graders:

> Coding is like doing crossword puzzles because one word in the wrong place affects the word that is going down or across that word. That relates to coding because if you do Scratch and put the wrong block, when you want to do something else, it turns into a disaster. When you do a crossword puzzle, at first it might be just experimenting and trying to fit the words in the squares. Same with coding. You have to experiment to see if the cat moves the way you want or not. At first, the crossword puzzle might look different or weird, but it turns out cool. With coding, it might look weird at first, but when it is finished, it is awesome!

Janice Mak is an instructional coach and teacher from Phoenix, Arizona. She helps her students learn through an interdisciplinary and "learning by doing" mindset. Read her blog and follow her on Twitter @jmakaz.

Students Create Tech Tutorials to Teach Each Other

By Nancy Watson

Empowered learner. Digital citizen. Knowledge constructor. Creative communicator. Our district has a program that helps students develop the skills they'll need for work and citizenship.

It's called CLICK – for Collaborate-Learn-Instruct-Create-Know – and it's a website of student-created technology tips, designed to bridge gaps in digital literacy.

Not all of today's students are the stereotypical "digital natives" who intuitively know their way around computers, apps and websites. Many don't have a lot of technology – or technology role models – at home, and they struggle with seemingly simple tech functions like logging into programs, managing files and sharing online documents.

On top of that, students often don't admit they lack the digital skills that their teachers assume they have, so they remain silent, and the digital divide widens.

Students Teaching Students

How do those students learn basic technology skills that many of us now take for granted? Teachers' agendas are already jam-packed with curricular content, and even the most organized and experienced educators often don't have the time to teach digital skills – or may not feel comfortable with their own tech abilities.

That's why we came up with a way to connect students who do have digital skills with those who do not, by encouraging tech-savvy students to create videos offering technology tips.

Students create brief explainer videos, graphics or other presentations that are captioned and then uploaded to the CLICK website.

And it's not only students who learn from the site. Anyone can access the site, and many adults who have explored CLICK for the first time say they, too, could probably learn something from the students' tips.

The CLICK website contains about 60 technology tips. CLICK's youngest contributor was a first-grader who made a short Chatterpix video about how to safely carry a Chromebook. A fourth grader contributed a screencast about using Google Voice Typing, and ended with a testimonial about how much Google Voice had helped him with his dyslexia. A group of middle schoolers created a presentation on "rules of texting." And there is a series of tips on the 3D modeling program Sketchup, produced by high school sophomores.

Students Take Charge of Website

At first, content creation relied on teachers and librarians who had either helped students create content or who used content submission to CLICK as part of a unit test or assignment.

Unsurprisingly, the biggest barrier to gathering content was time. While many educators had expressed a great deal of appreciation and support for the program, a project that does not directly correlate to their already rigorous job requirements was a tough sell.

That's why we made a shift that helped us reach our goal of giving students more ownership of CLICK. Enter Andrew and Caden, two students who attend our project-based learning high school, where each senior selects a project to work on all year. The principal of the school recommended them, and these young men have adopted CLICK as their capstone project.

Andrew and Caden are now actively involved with CLICK, working to improve the site and market it directly to their peers.

They created a CLICK Twitter account that now has nearly 500 followers. And they've embarked on a rebranding effort, improving the quality of the graphics and creating a professional style guide. They are using their own social media networks to promote the site and encourage other students to submit content directly to them.

Sharing Their Ideas with Educators

During the summer, Caden and Andrew presented about their interest and involvement in CLICK at a professional development event attended by over 350 teachers who were impressed by their poise and their vision.

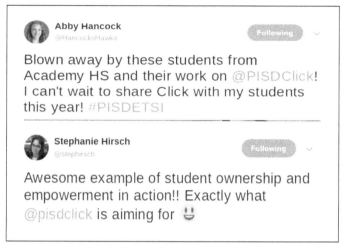

Figure 7.4. CLICK Twitter exchange.

The students encouraged teachers to contact them if they have a need for specific types of content and promised to find someone who would create those tutorials. They have plans to create tutorial series, much like Khan Academy.

The goal is for CLICK to become completely student-led and student-driven, growing organically by word of mouth among students and amplifying many student voices.

Students are Self-Taught and Self-Motivated

The students are also working to hand-code a new searchable website. Andrew has been coding the new site, with the help of his older brother who is studying computer science in college. Andrew said he's applying the coding skills he learned while participating on a school robotics team and he's learning as he goes.

When he and his brother get stumped, they reach out to other coders. "We search for answers to our problems on the internet," he said. "The online developer communities and documentation are probably the best resources."

Caden reports that he has always been interested in technology, particularly animation, robotics and, more recently, coding. He is in charge of marketing for the school robotics team. It was Caden's idea to award service hours for CLICK content production, and he wrote an announcement about that opportunity for the school's newsletter.

Tutorials in languages other than English are also encouraged, providing students who are new to the country — and their family members — with opportunities to learn tech skills, too.

"I love the concept of CLICK and I am so excited to be contributing to it, allowing it to grow and become more prominent, especially in our district," Caden said. "I hope that my contributions help achieve our goal: Giving anyone who has an idea an anchor to turn it into reality, all by their own hands."

Andrew added, "I'm excited to be working on CLICK. I hope it helps teachers and students get their foot in the door with less confusion and frustration. I hope it will be helpful to many."

Now there's some student voice.

Addressing the ISTE Standards for Students

Students who create the content for CLICK meet many of the indicators of the ISTE Standards for Students. For example, contributors are:

- Empowered Learners who leverage technology to take an active role in their learning and who understand the fundamental concepts of technology operations.

- Digital Citizens who engage in positive, safe, ethical and legal behavior.

- Knowledge Constructors who produce creative artifacts and make meaningful learning experiences for themselves and others.

- Innovative Designers who select and use digital tools to plan and manage a design process.

- Computational Thinkers who break problems into component parts.

- Creative Communicators who communicate clearly and express themselves for a variety of purposes using the platforms, tools, styles, formats
and digital media appropriate to their goals.

- Global Collaborators who use digital tools to connect with learners from
a variety of backgrounds and cultures.

This is an updated version of an article published on the ISTE Blog on September 9, 2017.

Nancy Watson is a district-level instructional technology specialist in Plano, Texas. Caden
and Andrew are seniors at Plano ISD's Academy High School. Watson serves as co-chair of
ISTE's Digital Citizenship PLN and is a Google for Education Certified Trainer and Innovator.
CLICK is her Innovator project.

5 Ways to Use Memes with Students

By Sharon Serano

I love memes and enjoy sharing them on Facebook, Twitter or even emailing
them to friends and coworkers. But until recently, it never occurred to me to use a
meme generator, a fun communication tool, in the classroom.

Figure 7.5. Student-created meme.

For those who aren't familiar with them, memes (pronounced meemz) are a cultural element or system of behavior that is passed from one individual to another. They are often represented by an image with a brief bold caption overlaid and shared on social media to capture attention or elicit a quick laugh.

One night while working hard on my lesson plans, my 14-year-old son decided to poke fun at me by sending me a text with the following meme that he created:

I had to laugh because it was true. And in that moment, I had an epiphany. What if I asked my students to create math-themed memes? The next day I set out the criteria for The Math Meme Project:

- The memes had to be their own creations.
- They could be about any algebra topic or about my class in general.
- Students could submit up to three.
- They could submit their creations to my school email.
- They had three weeks to turn them in.

Creating Memes

I told them to use one of the many meme-creation tools available to make their original memes. To get the ball rolling, I gave my students a handout with a few examples of math memes that had been published on the internet. Other than that, I didn't give them much direction because I wanted them to figure it out on their own.

Most students already had meme-making apps on their phones, but some students found a few websites online to create their submissions. The students were able to create these memes without any guidance from me.

If your students are younger, you may need to guide them through the process. The task of creating memes is simple once you find the right tool. Meme-creation apps are easy to find for laptops, tablets or smartphones. Search "meme-creation program" in the Apple App Store, Google Play or on your laptop, and many options will come up, including Meme Creator, Meme Generator and Quick Meme.

Warnings

It's important to preview any meme program before assigning it to the students to avoid fees or inappropriate content. Most meme-creation programs are free but some charge a small fee for an ad-free version.

Also, some meme-creation programs show other users' creations, some of which may be intended for a mature audience. Review the meme-creation homepage before inviting the students to the site. It might be best to avoid the webpage all together and just download the app onto devices before the lesson.

Surprising Results

By the time the due date arrived, I was delighted to find 38 students had turned in more than 100 memes! And I was struck with a revelation: Memes are a great educational device for teachers and students alike to promote clarity, pedagogy and humor.

I was so proud of my students' creations that I handpicked the best of them and included them — along with my son's and a few of my own — in a video that I posted on my YouTube channel and shared it with my students.

The Math Meme Project 2016 video became a hit and has been viewed thousands of times by people all over the world, including the U.S., Philippines, Hong Kong, South Africa, Malaysia, Australia, Austria, the United Kingdom, Ireland, Mexico, Canada, India, Honduras, Tunisia, Brazil, Germany, Turkey, Czechia, Philippines, Finland, Spain, Qatar, Romania, Belgium, and Indonesia.

I used the same project the following year as an extra credit opportunity with my math students. To introduce the project, I showed my classes the video from the previous year and encouraged them to create their own original memes. As a result, I received almost double the submissions from the year before. However I ran into new problems when creating the video for the Math Meme Project 2017, namely having to be more selective of the memes for video length and political leanings of the students.

This project has inspired other teachers to replicate this project with their classes. Bernadette Bogacki, a math teacher at Washington Township High School in Sewell, New Jersey, tried it with her Algebra 2 and Pre-Calculus students. She said the students enjoyed being able to think about math in a fun and imaginative way. "It helped to make the concepts more accessible in their minds — less stressful in a way. They really enjoyed collaborating with each other, sharing ideas and laughing in the process."

Using Memes as a Tool

Here are some ways you can use memes in your classroom.

Create class rules. Make a meme for each rule and post them in the classroom. As an alternative ice-breaking activity on the first day of school, ask students to create their own memes based on the rules and share the best ones with the class or post on the bulletin board.

Learn new vocabulary. Students can create memes to define or use new vocabulary. Display the word at the top, and place the definition or a sentence using the word below.

Figure 7.6. Class rules meme.

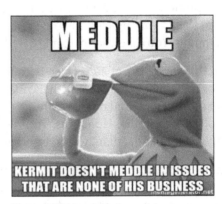

Figure 7.7. Vocabulary meme.

Identify the novel. Students can use memes to dramatize a point from a novel or short story. Teachers can break the class into groups and have each group create a meme from assigned chapters in a class novel.

Emphasize a historical event. Teachers and/or students can import an image into a meme-creation program and make their own meme with a witty subtitle.

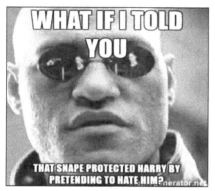

Figure 7.8. Meme from assigned reading.

Figure 7.9. Historical event meme.

Use as an ice breaker for the lesson. Teachers can create memes as a simple way to start the lesson with a laugh or ask the class to analyze the message. Students can also create memes as a way to review the material.

Figure 7.10. Ice breaker meme.

Aside from being a fun and novel way to get student engaged in content, these assignments can address the Creative Communicator standard, part of the ISTE Standards for Students, which expects students to communicate clearly and express themselves creatively for a variety of purposes using the platforms, tools, styles, formats and digital media appropriate to their goals.

Sharon Serano is a math teacher at Washington Township High School in Sewell, New Jersey. Follow her on Twitter @MrsSerano and check out her YouTube channel.

TPACK as a Tool for Professional Learning

By Teresa S. Foulger and David A. Slykhuis

A paint bucket with a nozzle inserted on the bottom of the can is hanging by a string, much like a pendulum. The paint drizzles onto a large sheet of butcher paper below. Then someone gives it a push. Simultaneously, someone pulls the paper along under the bucket at an even speed, creating a blue painted waveform on the paper. Over many trials, students begin to observe that the "push" is a variable that determines the amplitude of the wave, and the speed at which the paper is pulled is another variable that determines the wavelength and frequency of the waves.

This activity is an ideal instructional approach that helps middle school students anchor complex science concepts related to waveforms, amplitude, wavelength, frequency and energy. But ultimately, students are limited in their investigation of these phenomena due to lack of the time and materials necessary to systematically conduct the many trials needed to fully explore the variables.

To address this challenge after the original experiment, we used an iPad app to simulate the pendulum swing. In this way, students had unlimited opportunities for investigation. In the app, a mouse tracking ball is suspended over the screen in a manner similar to the way the paint bucket hung over the paper, and a student can start it swinging. The app then graphs the waveforms on the iPad screen, creating an illustration of the pathway of the mouse ball swing analogous to the paint on the paper.

This type of inquiry-based pedagogy allowed students to initially experience a real pendulum, then the app helped them to fully explore the variables of a pendulum swing. The teacher who designed this learning activity used an approach that required her to understand the interaction and interconnection among the technologies used, the pedagogical approach and the science content. The model is call TPACK, or technology, pedagogy and content knowledge.

TPACK as a Model

First introduced by Punya Mishra and Matthew Koehler, TPACK suggests that teachers require three separate and distinct knowledge bases for technology integration in their teaching: technological, pedagogical and content knowledge.

The model also accounts for the complex, multifaceted and situated nature of teacher practices that result when teachers call upon all three of these areas simultaneously as they seek to produce rich, technology-infused learning and teaching experiences.

The Practitioner's Guide to TPACK

To assist you with learning how to teach more effectively with technology, the National Technology Leadership Coalition created an online resource called The Practitioner's Guide to TPACK. The guide illustrates successful implementation of TPACK through video-based teaching cases and provides practical guidance for teachers and education leaders to use for professional development.

Exemplary cases in English language arts, science, mathematics and social studies at the elementary and secondary levels combine written explanations and videos of classroom experiences from both the student and teacher perspectives. Explicit connections to TPACK, examples of student work and assessment techniques are included to help make instructional planning more efficient for teachers. Also, designing instruction with attention to the affordances technology can provide will enhance student learning.

The Practitioner's Guide to TPACK includes the ebook along with a website to provide professional development aimed at supporting both preservice and inservice teachers.

Combined, these efforts support both preservice and inservice teachers in meaningful ways.

This is an updated version of an article that was published in Learning & Leading with Technology, August 2013.

Teresa S. Foulger, Ed.D., is an associate professor at Mary Lou Fulton Teachers College at Arizona State University. She is past president of the ISTE Teacher Educators Network.

David A. Slykhuis, Ph.D., is assistant dean at the University of Northern Colorado. He is also a past president of the Society of Information Technology and Teacher Education.

Arlene Borthwick, John K. Lee and Sarah McPherson also contributed to this article.

Resources

For more resources on digital learning tools and lessons, check out these resources.

Learning Transported: Augmented, Virtual and Mixed Reality for All Classrooms, by Jaime Donally. ISTE members save 25% at iste.org/TransportLearning.

No Fear Coding: Computational Thinking Across the K-5 Curriculum, by Heidi Williams. ISTE members save 25% at iste.org/NoFearCoding.

Members also enjoy access to the ISTE webinar "Integrating CS Across the Curriculum," at https://www.iste.org/resources/product?id=4122.